P9-CJF-248

PANORAMA

BUILDING PERSPECTIVE THROUGH READING

KATHLEEN F. FLYNN

DAPHNE MACKEY
LATRICIA TRITES

with DENA DANIEL, JOHN HOLLAND,
ELLEN KISSLINGER,
and ANASTASSIA TZOYTZOYRAKOS

OXFORD
UNIVERSITY PRESS

OXFORD
UNIVERSITY PRESS

198 Madison Avenue
New York, NY 10016 USA

Great Clarendon Street, Oxford OX2 6DP UK

Oxford University Press is a department of the University of Oxford.
It furthers the University's objective of excellence in research, scholarship,
and education by publishing worldwide in

Oxford New York

Auckland Cape Town Dar es Salaam Hong Kong Karachi
Kuala Lumpur Madrid Melbourne Mexico City Nairobi
New Delhi Shanghai Taipei Toronto

With offices in

Argentina Austria Brazil Chile Czech Republic France Greece
Guatemala Hungary Italy Japan Poland Portugal Singapore
South Korea Switzerland Thailand Turkey Ukraine Vietnam

OXFORD and OXFORD ENGLISH are registered trademarks of
Oxford University Press

© Oxford University Press 2006

Database right Oxford University Press (maker)

Developer: Angela M. Castro, English Language Trainers
Executive Publisher: Janet Aitchison
Editor: Phebe W. Szatmari
Art Director: Maj Hagsted
Senior Designer: Mia Gomez
Art Editor: Robin Fadool
Production Manager: Shanta Persaud
Production Controller: Zai Jawat Ali

ISBN : 978 0 19 430544 0

10 9 8 7 6 5 4 3

Printed in Hong Kong.

Acknowledgments:

Cover art:
Hans Hofmann
Combinable Wall I and II
1961
Oil on canvas
Overall: 84-1/2 x 112-1/2 inches
University of California, Berkeley Art Museum; Gift of the artist.

The publisher would like to thank the following for their permission to
reproduce photographs: Getty Images: MPI, v (Benjamin Banneker); Alamy: Steve
Bloom Images, v (eclipse); Index Stock Imagery, Inc.: Yvette Cardozo, 1; *Nunavut
Qajanartuk*, 1992, © Kenojuak Ashjevak/Canadian Museum of Civilization, 2;
Index Stock Imagery, Inc.: Yvette Cardozo, 5; Index Stock Imagery, Inc.: R.P.
Kingston, 8; Index Stock Imagery, Inc.: Great American Stock, 15; Schlesinger
Library/Radcliffe Institute/Harvard University, 16; Alamy: Andre Jenny, 19;
Courtesy Wikimedia: GFDL, 22; Courtesy Chicago Historical Society: Hedrich-
Blessing, 29; Getty Images: Slim Aarons/Stringer, 30; Farnsworth House ©
National Trust Historical Site, 33; Alamy: Dennis Cox, 36; Marian Anderson,
Courtesy Marian Anderson Collection, Rare Books & Manuscript Library,
University of Pennsylvania, 43; portrait of Marian Anderson, Courtesy National
Portrait Gallery, Smithsonian Institution, 44; Index Stock Imagery, Inc.: Bruce
Leighty, 47; Louis Armstrong © William P. Gotlieb/American Memory Collection/
Library of Congress, 50; *Quest for Quivera* by Norman Price © Bettmann/CORBIS,
57; Coronado portrait © Peter Hurd/Roswell Museum & Art Center, Roswell, New
Mexico, 58; americansouthwest.net: J.G. Crossley, 61; Index Stock Imagery, Inc.:
Fotopic, 64; Bettmann/CORBIS, 71; Alamy: POPPERFOTO, 72; Index Stock Imagery,
Inc.: Shubroto Chattopadhyay, 75; Time Life Pictures/Getty Images, 78; Illustrated
by Woodshed Productions, 85; Alamy: POPPERFOTO, 86; Index Stock Imagery,
Inc.: Erwin Bud Nielsen, 89; Index Stock Imagery, Inc.: Jeff Greenberg, 92; age
fotostock/SuperStock, 99; Courtesy Engines of Our Ingenuity: John H. Lienhard,
100; Alamy: PCL, 103; Index Stock Imagery, Inc.: Gary Conner, 106

The authors and publisher would like to acknowledge the following individuals
for their invaluable input during the development of this series:
Russell Frank, Pasadena City College, CA; Virginia Heringer, Pasadena City
College, CA; Barbara Howard, Daly Community College, IL; Maydell Jenks, Katy
Independent School District, TX; JoShell Koliva, Newcomer School, Ontario, CA;
Kathy Krokar, Truman Community College, IL; Catherine Slawson; University of
California, Davis, CA; Laura Walsh; City College of San Francisco, CA

CONTENTS

TO THE TEACHER

Welcome to *Panorama 2*, a reading skills text for high-beginning level students. *Panorama 2* combines high-interest reading passages from the content areas with a strong vocabulary strand and extensive reading skills practice to prepare students for the challenges of academic reading.

Each of the eight main units consists of three chapters, and each chapter has a thematically-linked reading passage. The first passage is about a person, the second about a related place, and the third about a related concept or event.

The book begins with an introductory unit, **Essential Reading Skills**, that presents and practices the core reading skills needed for academic success.

WHAT IS IN EACH UNIT?

Before You Read

This opening page introduces the theme of the unit. The questions and photographs can be used to activate students' prior knowledge and stimulate discussion before reading.

Prepare to Read

This section introduces the topic of the chapter. The questions and photographs encourage students to become engaged in the topic while sharing their own thoughts and experiences.

Word Focus

This matching activity introduces students to new or unfamiliar words that they will see in the reading passage. Students match the ten words with simple definitions.

Scan

This activity encourages students to make a prediction about a specific piece of information that appears in the passage. The aim is to motivate students to read the passages quickly as they try to find the answer.

Reading Passage

Each reading in Book 2 is about 500 words. The language is carefully graded using the Fry Readability Scale so that students gain confidence in reading; the average Fry Readability Score in *Panorama 2* is 6.0.

Check Your Comprehension

These multiple-choice questions check students' understanding of the passage. The questions include key skills such as understanding the main idea, reading for details, and reading for inference.

Vocabulary Review

This section reviews the vocabulary presented in the unit. It includes a wide variety of activities, such as **Words in Context** (filling in the gaps), **Which Meaning?** (choosing the definition that fits), **Wrong Word** (finding the word that doesn't fit the group), **Word Families** (choosing the part of speech that fits), and **Crossword Puzzles**. These activities help students use the new words as part of their active vocabulary.

Wrap It Up

This final section of the unit gives students the opportunity to discuss the theme of the unit with more confidence and holistic understanding. The last activity asks students to respond in writing about the passage they enjoyed the most. This activity reinforces what students have learned about the unit's theme.

The Essential Reading Skills: Answer Key and Explanations, a Vocabulary Index, and a list of Common Irregular Verbs can be found at the back of the book for easy reference.

An *Answer Key* and *Assessment CD-ROM with ExamView® Test Generator* are available for use with *Panorama 2*.

ESSENTIAL READING SKILLS

▲ Benjamin Banneker, 1731–1806

▲ A solar eclipse

PREVIEW AND PREDICT

Before you read, **preview** and **predict**. When you **preview**, you look at the photographs and the parts of a passage. When you **predict**, you make logical guesses about content.

A. Look at the photographs only. (Don't read the captions yet.) Answer these questions.

1. Describe what you see. _____

_____

2. What things can you guess, or **predict**, about the passage from the photographs? _____

_____

B. Now read the captions. Answer these questions.

1. What information do these captions tell you? _____

_____

2. Is Benjamin Banneker still living? How do you know? _____

_____

3. Have you heard of him? _____

4. Have you heard of a solar eclipse? What is it? _____

_____

✔ Look at page 113 for the explanations.

Benjamin Banneker: Astronomer

Benjamin Banneker was born in 1731 on a farm in Maryland. Banneker was African American. This was the time of **slavery** in the American **colonies**, but

5 Banneker's mother was a free woman. Because of this, Banneker was also free.

Banneker's grandmother taught him to read and write. He was always curious and wanted to know how things worked.

10 He saw his first watch at age 21. The young man took the watch apart and studied its design. Later, he decided to make his own clock. It took him two years to build it. He built the whole

15 clock from wood because that was the only material he had. Banneker's clock kept the correct time for over 40 years!

Banneker was also interested in **astronomy**, the study of the stars and

20 the planets. First, Banneker taught himself math. He borrowed books from friends. He used **instruments** such as the telescope to **observe** the stars and planets. He noticed how the

25 stars and planets moved. He also wrote his own calculations. That is how he predicted that a *solar* **eclipse** would happen on April 14, 1789. Many famous astronomers and mathematicians had

30 predicted a different date for this eclipse of the sun. Banneker correctly predicted the date of the eclipse. After that, other astronomers wanted to hear his ideas.

In 1791, Banneker began to publish

35 an **almanac**, a book with information about many everyday things. An almanac has information about the seasons and predictions about the weather. It also has the dates of future eclipses. An almanac

40 is usually published annually, or yearly.

Farmers needed to know when to plant their crops, and they used Banneker's almanac. Farmers trusted Banneker because he was a farmer, too.

45 They trusted his predictions about the weather.

Banneker knew many famous men of that time. He sent a copy of his almanac to Thomas Jefferson. Jefferson

50 saw that Banneker's predictions about eclipses were **accurate**. His predictions were correct because he made careful calculations. Jefferson admired Banneker's accuracy. Banneker also

55 knew George Washington. President Washington asked Banneker to work on a team to design the new capital city of the United States, Washington, D.C.

Banneker worked on the team as

60 a **surveyor**. Surveyors measure land. Banneker's numbers were always accurate. Pierre Charles L'Enfant was the head of the group. L'Enfant designed the **plan** for the new city. However,

65 L'Enfant often argued with George Washington. Washington was also a surveyor, and he questioned L'Enfant's calculations. L'Enfant became angry, so he quit and returned to France. He took

70 his plan with him.

Fortunately, Banneker was able to draw the plan from memory. He did it in just two days! He saved the project. You can still see his plan in Washington, D.C.

75 Even though Banneker drew the plan over 200 years ago, the city still has the same basic design today.

Banneker continued to study new things until his death in 1806. He was

80 a man of many interests and talents. Most importantly, Banneker was the first African American scientist, astronomer, and mathematician.

C. Read the title. Answer these questions.

1. Is the passage about a person, a place, or a thing? _____

2. What is the connection between the title and the photographs?

_____

3. What do you **predict** the passage will be about? _____

_____

D. Preview the passage. Look for words with special markings. Answer these questions.

1. How many words do you see in **boldface**? _____

2. How many words do you see in *italics*? _____

E. Look at the paragraphs. Answer these questions.

1. Which paragraph is the introduction? _____

2. Which paragraph is the conclusion? _____

✔ Look at page 113 for the explanations.

WHAT TO DO WHILE YOU READ

SKIMMING AND SCANNING

Sometimes, you need to read quickly to look for certain information. This is called **skimming** and **scanning**. You **skim** when you read quickly. As you **skim**, your eyes **scan** for specific information. Use the passage and these questions to practice.

A. To skim, let your eyes move quickly over the passage. Answer these questions by writing *Yes* or *No*.

Does it have dialogue? _____   Is it academic or professional? _____

Is it a story? _____   Does it have dates and events in a person's life? _____

Does it have technical vocabulary? _____   Is it a biography? _____

Does it have charts and diagrams? _____

B. Before you scan, decide what to look for. Find an example of each of these.

1. a word in **boldface** _____

2. a word in *italics* _____

3. a date _____

4. a number _____

5. a place name _____

6. a person's name _____

✔ Look at page 113 for the explanations.

C. Now answer this question.

Guess if this is true or false. Circle *a* or *b*.

Benjamin Banneker knew George Washington.

a. True   **b.** False

Scan the passage quickly to check your answer.

✔ Look at page 113 for the explanation.

MAIN IDEA

Every passage has a **main idea**. This is the most important topic or most general idea. Each paragraph also has a **main idea**. It is often in the first sentence, but not always.

D. Read the passage and answer the question. Circle your answer.

1. What is the main topic of the passage?
   A. the capital of the United States
   B. the first African American astronomer
   C. George Washington and Thomas Jefferson
   D. astronomy

✔ Look at page 114 for the explanation.

DETAIL

Every passage has many smaller, specific pieces of information that tell you more about the main idea. These are called **details**.

E. Read the passage and answer the questions. Circle your answers.

2. Benjamin Banneker was
   A. an astronomer
   B. a farmer
   C. a surveyor
   D. all of the above

3. What was special about the clock that Banneker made?
   A. It ran for 200 years.
   B. It was made completely of wood.
   C. It was the first clock made in the U.S.
   D. He gave it to Thomas Jefferson.

4. What did Banneker publish?
   A. a newspaper
   B. a book about Washington, D.C.
   C. an almanac
   D. a book about slavery

✔ Look at page 114 for the explanations.

INFERENCE

You can use details to make logical guesses. These logical guesses are called **inferences**. Often you have to think about information in different parts of the passage and then piece the information together.

F. Read the passage and answer the questions. Circle your answers.

5. Which of the following is **not** true?
   A. People admired Banneker's accuracy.
   B. Banneker understood L'Enfant's plan.
   C. Jefferson predicted a solar eclipse.
   D. Washington thought Banneker was a good surveyor.

6. What can we say about Banneker?
   A. He was a very good mathematician.
   B. He was born after slavery ended.
   C. He was the richest African American.
   D. His mother died when he was young.

✔ Look at page 115 for the explanations.

WORDS IN CONTEXT, PART 1

In every passage, you will often find words that are unfamiliar to you. Look for clues in the sentence or in nearby sentences to help you understand words in context.

G. Circle the answer with the same meaning as the words in boldface. Then underline the clues that helped you.

1. This was the time of **slavery** in the American colonies, but Banneker's mother was a free woman.
   - **A.** owning other people
   - **B.** freedom for all people
   - **C.** free education

2. He used instruments such as the telescope to **observe** the stars and planets. He noticed how the stars and planets moved.
   - **A.** name
   - **B.** look at
   - **C.** organize

3. Banneker's predictions about eclipses were **accurate**. His predictions were correct because he made careful calculations.
   - **A.** average
   - **B.** careless
   - **C.** correct

WORDS IN CONTEXT, PART 2

Sometimes the author gives a clue by defining words in context. The author might include a definition, an example, or a synonym. Sometimes the author defines a foreign word. Commas often set off definitions in context.

4. Underline the part of the sentence that defines *astronomy*. Circle the comma.
   Banneker was interested in astronomy, the study of the stars and the planets.

5. Underline the example of an instrument.
   He used instruments such as the telescope to observe the stars.

6. Underline the synonyms in this sentence. Circle the comma.
   An almanac is usually published annually, or yearly.

7. Underline the phrase that means the same as the term *solar*.
   That is how he predicted that a *solar* eclipse would happen on April 14, 1789. Many . . . had predicted a different date for this eclipse of the sun.

✔ Look at page 115 for the explanations.

UNIT 1

ANTHROPOLOGY
THE INUIT

▲ An Inuit in front of a winter home

BEFORE YOU READ

Answer these questions.

1. The person in this photo is an Inuit. What do you know about the Inuit people?

2. What do you think life is like in the Arctic?

3. Do you think you could live in such a cold climate?

1

CHAPTER 1

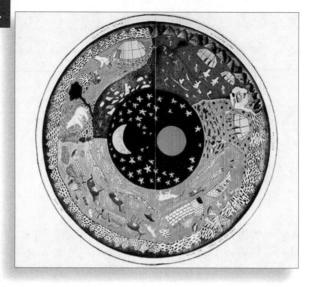

Nunavut Qajanartuk (Our Beautiful Land) by Kenojuak, 1992

PREPARE TO READ

Discuss these questions.

1. Describe what is in the image.

2. What do you think of the design?

WORD FOCUS

Match the words with their definitions.

A.

1. bead ___   **a.** an idea
2. carve ___   **b.** a small ball of wood, glass, or plastic with a hole in the middle
3. concept ___   **c.** a job or an activity for which you need skill
4. craft ___   **d.** cut wood or stone to make an object
5. exist ___   **e.** be real; be found in the real world

B.

1. form ___   **a.** a large picture that is painted on a wall
2. mural ___   **b.** things that people need to use in their daily lives
3. remote ___   **c.** far away from where other people live
4. sew ___   **d.** join cloth using a needle and thread
5. supplies ___   **e.** create

SCAN

Guess if this is true or false. Circle *a* or *b*.

The artist Kenojuak came from a family of artists.

a. True   **b.** False

Scan the passage quickly to check your answer.

Kenojuak: An Inuit Artist

The Inuit artist Kenojuak grew up in a **remote** Inuit village in northern Canada. As a young girl growing up in the 1930s, she never dreamed of being
5 an artist. In fact, in the Inuit language, there isn't even a word for art!

As a child, Kenojuak lived with her grandparents. In this remote place, children had to entertain themselves.
10 In the summer, Kenojuak spent a lot of time chasing birds and watching wildlife. Her grandmother taught her to **sew** sealskins. They sold the sealskins to a trading company.

15 At 19, Kenojuak's mother and stepfather arranged for her to marry a hunter named Jonniebo. At first, she didn't want to marry him, but over time she grew to love him. They had three
20 children, but life wasn't easy. Their two daughters died from food poisoning. To help them, another family adopted their son. This was a common custom in Inuit life.

25 Life was difficult for all the Inuit people. It was hard to **exist** so far north and hard to make a living. When Kenojuak was 25, a nurse came to her village. The nurse found that Kenojuak
30 was very ill with tuberculosis. Kenojuak had to spend the next three years at a hospital far away in Quebec City. In a **crafts** program at the hospital, she started to make crafts with **beads**. When
35 she got better, Kenojuak returned to her home. She continued to work with beads.

The Inuit had a different **concept** of art. Art was a social activity. Men
40 **carved** small sculptures out of a soft rock called soapstone. They did this just to entertain themselves. Women made designs in beads and sewed them onto clothing. It was people outside the Inuit
45 culture who saw and appreciated the beauty of Inuit art. James Houston was one such person. He was an artist from Toronto. He encouraged Kenojuak to try drawing and gave her some **supplies**.
50 She began to draw her own designs to decorate bags made of sealskin. She drew what she knew best—birds and animals. Houston introduced Kenojuak to a group of people who were doing
55 similar work in another village, Cape Dorset.

With James Houston's help, the artists **formed** the Cape Dorset Cooperative. They made prints of their work and
60 sold the prints in a catalogue. One of the most popular items in the catalogue was one of Kenojuak's designs. This success changed Kenojuak's life. Inuit art became very popular, and Kenojuak
65 became known throughout Canada. Her work was shown in galleries and museums. Her prints were even used on postage stamps. In 1970, she and her husband traveled to Osaka, Japan, where
70 they drew a **mural** for the 1970 World's Fair.

Kenojuak became famous, but she remains a part of the Inuit community. She spends time with her family at the
75 family's summer camp just as she always has. Kenojuak finally thinks of her work as art. But she considers it just one part of her life, not the most important thing. She is still an Inuit first and an artist
80 second.

Read the passage again and answer the questions. Circle your answers.

MAIN IDEA

1. What is the main topic of the passage?
   A. Inuit art
   B. Inuit artists
   C. one Inuit artist
   D. Inuit life

DETAIL

2. Why did Kenojuak spend time in Quebec?
   A. She was sick.
   B. She was in a crafts program.
   C. Her family moved there.
   D. She went to school there.

3. How many children did Kenojuak and Jonniebo have?
   A. one
   B. two
   C. three
   D. four

4. Which of the following is true?
   A. Inuit men made small carvings.
   B. Inuit women sewed designs in beads.
   C. Kenojuak decorated sealskin bags.
   D. all of the above

5. What did Kenojuak design?
   A. catalogues
   B. soapstone sculptures
   C. prints with birds and animals
   D. all of the above

6. What is most important to Kenojuak?
   A. her art
   B. her family and community
   C. being famous
   D. helping the Cape Dorset artists

INFERENCE

7. James Houston
   A. had Inuit relatives
   B. was very enthusiastic about Inuit art
   C. lived in Quebec City
   D. knew Kenojuak as a child

8. Why didn't the Inuit have a word for art?
   A. They never did anything artistic.
   B. Their language was too new.
   C. They didn't like the idea of art.
   D. Creating art was just part of everyday life.

CHAPTER 2

An Inuit fishing on the ice

PREPARE TO READ

Discuss these questions.

1. Describe what you see in the photo.
2. What do you know about how the Inuit lived in the Arctic?

WORD FOCUS

Match the words with their definitions.

A.

1. adapt ___   **a.** not pleasant
2. harsh ___   **b.** a small bag, usually for carrying things
3. hearth ___   **c.** continuing for a long time or forever
4. permanent ___   **d.** a place for an open fire inside a house
5. pouch ___   **e.** change behavior because the situation has changed

B.

1. rare ___   **a.** a building
2. skin ___   **b.** not found or seen very often
3. structure ___   **c.** the natural outer covering of an animal
4. suit ___   **d.** continue to live or exist after a difficult or dangerous situation
5. survive ___   **e.** be convenient or acceptable for somebody or something

SCAN

Guess the answer. Circle *a* or *b*.

What is the name for a boat built by the Inuit?

a. canoe   **b.** kayak

Scan the passage quickly to check your answer.

Life in the Arctic

The Arctic is sometimes called "the land of the midnight sun." This is because in mid-June, the sun is still shining at midnight. In contrast, for
5 several months in the winter, it is dark almost 24 hours a day. In winter, the temperature can be as cold as –50 degrees F (–46 C). Even in the summer, hardly anything grows this far north. It
10 is difficult for most people to imagine living in the Arctic.

The Inuit, however, have managed to **survive** in this **harsh** environment for thousands of years. In order to survive,
15 they **adapted** their way of living. Their housing, clothing, and transportation exactly **suited** the conditions in the Arctic.

Since nothing grew in the Arctic, the
20 Inuit hunted and fished. In the winter, they hunted for large animals such as polar bears and seals on the ice. In the summer, they fished and hunted for whales. The Inuit used every part of
25 the animal for food, to make clothes, to build boats and houses, and even to provide heat.

Most Inuit lived in different places and in different types of **structures**,
30 depending on the time of the year. In their **permanent** villages, the Inuit built houses. They dug the floors below ground level and lined the sides with rocks. Then they used rocks, earth, and
35 animal **skins** to cover the houses. They built **hearths** to keep the houses warm and tunnels to enter the houses when the snow was deep.

The Inuit left their villages to hunt
40 and fish. In their winter camps, they built houses from blocks of snow and ice. In their summer camps, they used tents made of animal skins.

The Inuit also used animal skins for
45 their clothing. They made warm winter boots with layers of skin and fur. They wore parkas, a type of coat with a hood to cover the head. Women with babies wore a special parka, an *amoat,* with a
50 hood like a **pouch** so they could carry their babies. In the winter, one parka was not enough. The Inuit wore inner and outer parkas as well as pants and mittens made from animal skins.

55 The Inuit developed interesting ways of traveling in this environment. They used teams of dogs to pull heavy sleds over the ice and snow. There was no wood to use for boats, so the Inuit built
60 boats covered with skins. The Inuit built *kayaks,* narrow boats for just one or two people. They also built larger boats called *umiaks.*

Nature was harsh, but the Inuit
65 adapted successfully. In recent years, however, the Arctic has changed. The climate is warmer, and there is less ice. Hunters have to go a long way to find seals, and whales are **rare** today. The
70 warmer climate brings more storms, so it is more dangerous to be on the water.

With less hunting and fishing, the Inuit are left with few ways to make a living. The Inuit were successful in
75 Arctic conditions for 10,000 years, but the next 50 years may be a challenge.

Read the passage again and answer the questions. Circle your answers.

MAIN IDEA

1. What is the main topic of this passage?
   A. the excitement of Arctic life
   B. famous Inuit people
   C. how the Inuit built houses in the summer and winter
   D. ways the Inuit managed to survive in the Arctic

DETAIL

2. What is an *amoat*?
   A. a boat for more than one person
   B. a parka with a very large hood
   C. a house with a tunnel for entering through the snow
   D. a type of animal

3. What did the Inuit use animal skins for?
   A. houses
   B. clothing
   C. boats
   D. all of the above

4. Which of these is **not** a reason the Inuit hunt and fish less?
   A. There are fewer whales.
   B. There are more storms.
   C. They prefer food from stores.
   D. The climate is warmer.

5. Which of the following describes Inuit houses?
   A. They were built on the ice in the summer.
   B. They were built on sleds.
   C. The floors were built above ground level.
   D. They were built with rocks, skins, and earth.

6. Why did the Inuit wear two parkas in the winter?
   A. because of the cold
   B. so they could carry their children
   C. so they could use one for a tent
   D. to keep their feet warm and dry

INFERENCE

7. What is the biggest challenge for the Inuit today?
   A. surviving in the Arctic weather
   B. finding jobs
   C. hunting and fishing
   D. making boats

8. Why did the Inuit develop unique boats, houses, and clothing?
   A. They are very artistic people.
   B. They liked to invent new things.
   C. They copied other boats, houses, and clothing.
   D. They had to figure out how to survive in a harsh place.

CHAPTER 3

◀ A dogsled

PREPARE TO READ

Discuss these questions.

1. How do you think the Inuit felt when they met outsiders?

2. What do you think other Canadians thought about the Inuit?

WORD FOCUS

Match the words with their definitions.

A.

1. balance ___   **a.** need somebody to provide something
2. contact ___   **b.** the act of producing power
3. depend on ___   **c.** meeting, talking to, or writing to somebody else
4. generation ___   **d.** separate, alone, or apart from others
5. isolated ___   **e.** when different or opposite things are equal

B.

1. original ___   **a.** not existing in large quantities
2. scarce ___   **b.** the part that many people believe exists after the body is dead
3. share ___   **c.** first; earliest
4. spirit ___   **d.** a piece of equipment used to catch animals
5. trap ___   **e.** have, use, or pay for something with someone else

SCAN

Guess if this is true or false. Circle *a* or *b*.

The Inuit started having contact with outsiders about 200 years ago.

a. True   **b.** False

Scan the passage quickly to check your answer.

Life among the Inuit

The native people who live in the Arctic regions across North America, eastern Siberia, and Greenland are called the Inuit. The name *Inuit* means
5 "the people." In the past, these people were called Eskimos. The Inuit first came to the North American continent at least 10,000 years ago. At that time, sea levels were lower, and there was a
10 land bridge between Alaska in North America and Asia. When this land bridge existed, people could move between the two continents.

Today, there are 13 different groups
15 of Inuit. Each group has slightly different languages and art styles, but the groups **share** many customs and cultural values.

In the harsh northern climate, the Inuit people developed a strong sense of
20 community. Life was difficult, and the Inuit people **depended on** each other. Sharing was an important value. Men hunted large animals together in groups, and families often shared food and the
25 warmth of a fire.

The Inuit believed in the **balance** of life with nature. They hunted and killed only the animals they needed in order to live. They believed that animals had
30 **spirits**. The Inuit customs showed their respect for the animal spirits.

Many of the Inuit lived in small, **isolated** villages in northern Canada. For thousands of years, the Inuit had
35 almost no **contact** with outsiders. This changed about 350 years ago. First came the explorers and the whalers. Then came the traders. The traders wanted animal furs and goods such as whale oil
40 and ivory. In exchange, the Inuit wanted iron tools, knives, and guns. The Inuit began to hunt with the guns, and they began to use modern **traps** to catch animals for fur. Over time, the animals
45 became **scarcer**. A way of life that had existed for thousands of years was changing.

In the mid 1900s the Canadian government became more involved
50 with the Inuit people. They counted how many Inuit were living in Canada. The government started to give the Inuit people the same health care and education that other Canadians had. The
55 government gave each Inuit a surname even though last names weren't a part of traditional Inuit culture.

In the 1960s and 1970s, the Inuit became politically active. Over time,
60 the Inuit had lost much of their land. Companies had taken land for oil exploration and power **generation**. The Inuit wanted their land back. They also wanted a voice in decisions about their
65 people. In 1999, Canada gave much of their **original** land back to the Inuit and formed a new territory. It is called "Nunavut." In Inuit, this means "our land."

70 In the 21st century, life has changed for the Inuit. Most Inuit no longer live in small villages. As their old ways of life have disappeared, many Inuit have moved to larger towns or cities to look
75 for jobs. Life was difficult before, but now the Inuit face a new challenge— how to keep their traditional customs and language in a modern world.

Read the passage again and answer the questions. Circle your answers.

MAIN IDEA

1. What is the main topic of the passage?
   A. the culture and traditions of the Inuit
   B. the way the Inuit crossed the land bridge
   C. the political activities of the Inuit
   D. the geography of Canada, Siberia, and Greenland

DETAIL

2. What was the most important value in Inuit culture?
   A. hunting
   B. sharing
   C. isolation
   D. political independence

3. Which of these did the Inuit **not** get from the traders?
   A. modern traps
   B. knives
   C. guns
   D. furs

4. What changed after the traders came?
   A. The Inuit trapped animals for the fur trade.
   B. The Inuit killed only the animals they needed to survive.
   C. The Inuit established a balance with nature.
   D. The Inuit hunted large animals in groups.

5. When did the Inuit first come to North America?
   A. more than 10,000 years ago
   B. 350 years ago
   C. in the 1960s and 1970s
   D. 3,000 years ago

6. What is Nunavut?
   A. the most common Inuit surname
   B. the name the Inuit called the traders
   C. the name of the new Canadian territory
   D. the name of a famous Inuit hunter

INFERENCE

7. Animals became scarcer because of
   A. changes in the way the Inuit hunted
   B. change in the length of day
   C. diseases that killed the animals
   D. modern foods

8. Why did the Canadian government form a new territory?
   A. to give the Inuit better health care and education
   B. to get the government's land back
   C. to give the Inuit more control over their original land
   D. to encourage political activity

VOCABULARY REVIEW

WHICH MEANING?

From Chapter 1: *Kenojuak: An Inuit Artist*

1. What does *fair* mean in the following sentence?

   > In 1970, she and her husband went to Osaka, Japan, where they drew a mural for the 1970 World's Fair.

   A. fair *(adjective)* treating each person equally
   B. fair *(noun)* a public event with exhibits and entertainment
   C. fair *(adjective)* the opposite of dark

From Chapter 2: *Life in the Arctic*

2. What does *lined* mean in the following sentence?

   > They dug the floors below ground level and lined the sides with rocks.

   A. lined *(verb)* drew parallel marks on a surface
   B. lined *(adjective)* having an extra layer of material under the surface
   C. lined *(verb)* put around the inside of a structure

From Chapter 3: *Life among the Inuit*

3. What does *power* mean in the following sentence?

   > Companies had taken the land for oil exploration and power generation.

   A. power *(noun)* electricity
   B. power *(verb)* to supply energy to something
   C. power *(noun)* the ability to do something

WRONG WORD

One word in each group does not fit. Circle the word.

1. trap	mural	hunt	kill
2. remote	isolated	far	spirit
3. craft	beads	sew	hunt
4. depend on	share	trap	help
5. die	survive	exist	live
6. hearth	structure	tunnel	craft

WORDS IN CONTEXT

Fill in the blanks with words from each box.

beads	carve	form	isolated	rare

1. That type of bird is _____ in this part of the world. It's not usually found so far north.
2. The men _____ beautiful sculptures out of stone.
3. The Inuit live in a very _____ part of the world.
4. She sewed _____ on the parka in a beautiful design.
5. They decided to _____ a cooperative to sell their crafts.

adapt	contact	hearth	mural	trap

6. The room was cold, but it was warm next to the _____.
7. It took a long time to paint the _____ on the side of the building.
8. The design of the kayak is one of the ways the Inuit managed to _____ in the Arctic.
9. The hunter caught the animal in a _____.
10. In the 1700s, the Inuit started to have _____ with traders and whalers.

balance	depend on	harsh	skins	survive

11. Life in the Arctic is very _____. Winters are extremely cold.
12. The Inuit tried to maintain a _____ with nature.
13. They sewed clothes out of animal _____.
14. The Inuit people had to _____ each other to survive.
15. It was difficult to _____ in the Arctic.

WORD FAMILIES

Fill in the blanks with words from each box.

generate *(verb)*	generator *(noun)*	generation *(noun)*

1. How much electricity does that power plant _____?
2. There was no electricity, so they used a _____.

| origin (noun) | originate (verb) | original (adjective) |

3. The _____ house wasn't in good shape, so they tore it down and built a new one.

4. The _____ of many English words is Latin.

| supply (verb) | supplies (noun) | supplier (noun) |

5. The hunters brought _____ with them on the boat.

6. Two companies _____ most of their food and clothing.

WRAP IT UP

DISCUSS THE THEME

Read these questions. Discuss your answers with a partner.

The Inuit were different from most people in Canada in their customs, values, and types of skills. Think of groups you know of in other countries who were also different from others.

- Who were the people in the group?
- Where were they from originally?
- What customs did they have that were different?
- When did they first have contact with other people? How are/were they treated?
- What challenges have they had?

RESPOND IN WRITING

Look back at the unit and choose the passage you enjoyed the most. Read it again. Write a short summary of the passage.

_____

_____

_____

_____

_____

What do you think is the most interesting thing about this passage, and why? Write a short paragraph.

_____

_____

_____

_____

_____

_____

_____

BUSINESS
THE FOOD INDUSTRY

▲ A large selection of food

BEFORE YOU READ

Answer these questions.

1. What was your favorite food when you were a child?

2. What is your favorite food now?

3. Who is the best cook you know?

CHAPTER 1

Julia Child, 1912-2004

PREPARE TO READ

Discuss these questions.

1. Do you like to cook? Why or why not?
2. Can you name any famous chefs?

WORD FOCUS

Match the words with their definitions.

A.
1. accomplish ___   **a.** special, well-prepared meals
2. exquisite ___   **b.** complete successfully
3. gourmet ___   **c.** make someone feel that he/she can do something
4. inspire ___   **d.** cheerful
5. joyful ___   **e.** of great beauty

B.
1. legacy ___   **a.** impossible to understand
2. masterpiece ___   **b.** a person's life accomplishments
3. proverb ___   **c.** a work of great skill
4. unimaginable ___   **d.** done by all people in the world
5. universal ___   **e.** a saying

SCAN

Guess of this is true or false. Circle *a* or *b*.

French food inspired Julia Child to become a chef.

a. True   **b.** False

Scan the passage quickly to check your answer.

Julia Child: Food Makes the World a Better Place

Our world is made up of many different cultures, languages, customs, and traditions. Communication between cultures can be difficult. However, there is one thing that people around the world have in common: food. Food is a **universal** language. People everywhere enjoy eating good food with their friends and loved ones. An old Irish **proverb** says, "Laughter is brightest where food is best." Good food makes people happier and brings them closer together. This simple truth has **inspired** many of the world's greatest chefs. One such famous chef was Julia Child.

Julia Child was born August 15, 1912. Her mother didn't know how to cook very well, so Julia didn't learn how to cook from her mother. However, Julia's mother loved to entertain guests in their home. From her mother, Julia learned the joy of sharing meals with family and friends. Julia believed that one of the most wonderful things in life is dining together with loved ones.

Julia discovered the art of cooking during one of her trips to France in 1948. The food there was **exquisite**. This inspired Julia to learn about French cooking. At that time, in the United States, a typical home-cooked meal included salad, green peas, roast beef, and apple pie. French cooking was something foreign and **unimaginable** in the average American home. Julia changed that forever.

Julia's cookbooks and television shows taught Americans how to cook **gourmet** meals. Most importantly, Julia showed people how to have fun in the kitchen.

Her **joyful** personality and sense of humor attracted millions of viewers. Julia was never afraid to speak her mind. She loved good food, and she disliked diets. Diets, she believed, do not allow people to enjoy their food.

Julia's success was enormous. She hosted eight television shows and wrote about a dozen cookbooks. Many of the shows were filmed in the kitchen of her home in Cambridge, Massachusetts. Guests from all over the world visited her there to cook and share a meal. She was one of the world's most-loved chefs.

Julia lived a long life doing what she loved best: cooking and teaching others to create **masterpieces** in the kitchen. So many people thank Julia for inspiring them to enjoy meals together with family and friends. That's what Julia was able to **accomplish**. She taught people how to cook gourmet meals to please their loved ones. She encouraged others to take pleasure in what they eat. Thanks to Julia, more people found joy in cooking and sharing great meals with family and friends. Julia and her cooking succeeded in bringing people closer together.

When Julia retired, her famous kitchen in Cambridge became part of the Smithsonian Institution's collection. Her pots and pans hang in this famous museum exactly as they did in her kitchen. This great chef was herself an institution. People everywhere loved Julia Child. On her death in August 2004 at the age of 91, the world lost a much-loved chef. Her **legacy**, however, will live on for years to come.

Read the passage again and answer the questions. Circle your answers.

MAIN IDEA

1. What is the main topic of the passage?
   A. French food
   B. American food
   C. Julia Child
   D. cooking shows

DETAIL

2. Julia Child decided to learn more about cooking because
   A. of television
   B. of a trip to France
   C. she liked roast beef
   D. she wanted to be famous

3. What made Julia's television shows so popular?
   A. her cheerful personality
   B. her numerous cookbooks
   C. her apple pie
   D. her enormous kitchen

4. Why was Julia so popular?
   A. She pleased her friends and family.
   B. She lived a long life.
   C. She taught people to cook well and enjoy it.
   D. She wrote a dozen cookbooks.

5. Which of the following is **not** true?
   A. Julia Child changed the way Americans cooked.
   B. Julia Child's mother taught Julia how to cook.
   C. Julia Child's kitchen is in a museum.
   D. Julia Child lived a long and happy life.

6. Julia Child disliked diets because
   A. she thought people were thin enough
   B. she was retired
   C. they don't let people enjoy food
   D. her mother also disliked them

INFERENCE

7. Julia enjoyed
   A. writing cookbooks
   B. sharing meals with family and friends
   C. creating food masterpieces
   D. all of the above

8. What did Julia think about good food?
   A. Good food can make a chef famous.
   B. Good food makes people happier.
   C. Good food is only gourmet food.
   D. Good food is about impressing people.

CHAPTER 2

Street signs in Hershey, Pennsylvania

PREPARE TO READ

Discuss these questions.

1. Where is the best place to visit in the world?

2. What are some things people usually do on vacation?

WORD FOCUS

Match the words with their definitions.

A.
1. aroma ___   **a.** someone who starts something
2. charity ___   **b.** help for those in need
3. community ___   **c.** kind, giving
4. founder ___   **d.** a nice smell
5. generous ___   **e.** a group of people living together in one place

B.
1. individually ___   **a.** a place with a mineral spring or bath
2. recipe ___   **b.** one of a kind
3. souvenir ___   **c.** something to remember a place you visit
4. spa ___   **d.** separately
5. unique ___   **e.** a list of ingredients and instructions to make food

SCAN

Guess the answer. Circle *a* or *b*.

How many tourists visit the Chocolate Town every year?

a. one million   **b.** three million

Scan the passage quickly to check your answer.

The Sweetest Place on Earth

Many of the world's famous cities are known by some special name. Paris is known as the "City of Light." Los Angeles is called the "film capital" of the world. Hong Kong is the "Wall Street of Asia." One small city in Pennsylvania may be the sweetest place on Earth. That is the town of Hershey. Hershey is known as the "Chocolate Town." It is named after Milton Hershey. He was the **founder** of the largest chocolate factory in the world.

Milton Hershey built his first candy factory in the early 1900s. At the time, Hershey was developing a **recipe** for milk chocolate. Eventually he succeeded. Hershey was also the first to produce **individually** wrapped chocolate bars. Over time, his factory grew and produced more and more types of chocolate. To this day, Hershey's chocolate factory is the largest in the world.

Hershey used his success to give back to the **community**. He built a town around the factory for his employees. He gave streets fun names like Chocolate Avenue. He built schools, parks, and shops. This **generous** man gave millions of dollars to **charity**. Hershey made sure that the schools provided quality education. He built an amusement park with rides, trains for the children, and a swimming pool. Over the years, the town grew. People from near and far came to visit this special town. Its fame and beauty continue to attract tourists to this day. Every year, close to three million tourists visit the Chocolate Town.

Today, visitors to the city can enjoy a variety of attractions and activities. The Hershey chocolate factory offers tours. Visitors can learn all about chocolate and how it is made. A gift shop sells all kinds of chocolate and toys made to look like chocolate. Even if you don't buy a **souvenir**, there is one thing that is impossible to forget: the wonderful **aroma** of fresh chocolate everywhere. In this special place even the streetlights are shaped like chocolates.

Another attraction is the Hotel Hershey. It has a **unique spa** where guests can enjoy a variety of special treatments. The spa treatments all have one thing in common: chocolate. Guests can take a "whipped cocoa bath." Instead of an ordinary bubble bath, guests bathe in foaming chocolate milk. To relax tired muscles, guests can choose a "cocoa massage." This treatment uses massage oils made from chocolate. Guests can enjoy cocoa beauty treatments of every type imaginable. And, of course, the restaurant offers not only chocolate desserts but also other dishes with chocolate as an ingredient.

Visitors have enjoyed the attractions of Chocolate Town for almost a century. One man's dream in the early 1900s became reality. Milton Hershey created some of the most popular chocolate products in the United States. He was a giving and generous man, and he was able to help many people. The town of Hershey offers unique attractions for those who visit. Chocolate Town is surely one of the sweetest places on Earth.

Read the passage again and answer the questions. Circle your answers.

MAIN IDEA

1. What is the main topic of this passage?
   A. famous cities around the world
   B. Hershey chocolates
   C. the Chocolate Town
   D. Milton Hershey

DETAIL

2. What was Milton Hershey developing when he built his factory?
   A. a recipe for milk chocolate
   B. attractions for the community
   C. an amusement park
   D. public structures

3. What is true about the chocolate factory today?
   A. It offers tours.
   B. It is the largest in the world.
   C. It has an aroma of chocolate.
   D. all of the above

4. What is unique about the spa?
   A. the chocolate employees
   B. the individual bars
   C. the souvenirs
   D. the chocolate treatments

5. Which of the following did Milton Hershey **not** do?
   A. develop a recipe for milk chocolate
   B. make the first individually wrapped chocolates
   C. write the first chocolate cookbook
   D. found the largest chocolate factory in the world

6. What types of souvenirs can you buy in Hershey?
   A. toys that look like chocolate
   B. swimming pools filled with chocolate
   C. whipped cocoa baths
   D. street signs from around the world

INFERENCE

7. What is true about Milton Hershey?
   A. He liked to cook.
   B. He wanted to be famous.
   C. He cared about his employees.
   D. He did not pay his employees very well.

8. Why is Hershey a popular travel spot?
   A. It has the best amusement park in the world.
   B. It is a unique place.
   C. It is made of chocolate.
   D. It has a spa.

CHAPTER 3

Science is changing the foods we eat.

PREPARE TO READ

Discuss these questions.

1. What are some foods that are good for your health?

2. What are some foods that are bad for your health? Which do you prefer to eat?

WORD FOCUS

Match the words with their definitions.

A.
1. allergy ___   **a.** something that causes change or progress
2. alter ___   **b.** a bad reaction to certain foods
3. crop ___   **c.** created, changed by scientists
4. development ___   **d.** change in some small way
5. engineered ___   **e.** all the food grown at one time or place

B.
1. genetic ___   **a.** the effect of what we eat on our health
2. nutrition ___   **b.** a type of disease
3. opponent ___   **c.** stopping the action of something; not affected by something
4. resistant ___   **d.** relating to genes
5. virus ___   **e.** someone who is against something

SCAN

Choose the correct answer.

What crop was almost destroyed by a virus in Hawaii?

a. apple   **b.** papaya

Scan the text quickly to check your answer.

What did you have for lunch today?

Many people are careful about what they eat. **Nutrition** and a healthy lifestyle are important to people around the world. A good balance of nutritious
5 foods is important for a healthy body. Most people agree that fruits and vegetables are part of a balanced diet. However, some people believe that the fruits and vegetables you eat may be
10 dangerous for your health.

Today, many foods are genetically **engineered** (GE). GE foods have slowly become a part of our diet. GE foods are an example of how science is trying to
15 improve nature. Scientists use a special process to put new **genetic** information into a plant. In other words, the plant's DNA, or genetic code, changes. For instance, to protect a plant from a
20 certain **virus**, scientists can put a gene into the plant to make it more **resistant** to the virus.

An example is the Hawaiian papaya. According the U.S. Food and Drug
25 Administration (FDA), in the mid-1990s, the entire papaya **crop** in Hawaii was almost destroyed by a virus. There was nothing farmers could do. Researchers tried genetic engineering.
30 They put small pieces of the DNA for the virus into the papaya plant. This **altered** the plant's genetic code. This change resulted in a papaya that was resistant to the virus.

35 **Developments** like these seem positive. Why then has there been a worldwide negative reaction to GE foods? Why are so many organizations, nutritionists, and health professionals
40 concerned about GE foods?

The answer is simple: Genetically changed plants are no longer the same. Think of something like GE tomatoes. They may be larger and juicier, but
45 they may contain DNA from plants such as nuts or even from animals such as fish. **Opponents** of GE foods say that the greatest danger is for people **allergic** to substances such as nuts or
50 fish. That plump tomato could cause an allergic reaction—possibly even death for someone with severe allergies. Yet a person with allergies might never know that the tomato contained the substance.

55 Some scientists and government agencies feel that GE foods are safe for everyone. They believe that testing ensures that these foods are safe. However, those who oppose GE foods
60 want labels on all GE food. They want the label to say that the food is a GE food. That way, people will know what they are buying. Those who support GE foods claim there is no need for labeling.
65 They say that these foods aren't very different from foods grown the usual way.

Clearly, this is an ongoing battle. On one hand, scientists are developing GE
70 foods that last longer and are tastier and more nutritious. Supporters of GE foods even believe that GE foods can be the solution to world hunger. On the other hand, a growing number of people
75 worry that GE foods may be dangerous to our health. They demand testing and labeling of these foods. You may want to think about all this the next time you sit down to enjoy your crisp, green salad!

Read the passage again and answer the questions. Circle your answers.

MAIN IDEA

1. What is the main topic of this passage?
    A. foods people have for lunch
    B. the Hawaiian papaya
    C. FDA foods
    D. GE foods

DETAIL

2. What is true about GE foods?
    A. Their genetic code is changed.
    B. They are very rare.
    C. Everyone agrees they are safe.
    D. all of the above

3. What do some government agencies think about GE foods?
    A. They are dangerous.
    B. They are completely safe.
    C. They are tastier than regular foods.
    D. They will solve world hunger.

4. What do some people want to do?
    A. add new DNA to all foods
    B. put labels on GE foods
    C. stop all research on GE foods
    D. make everyone eat GE foods

5. What does FDA stand for?
    A. Food and Diet Association
    B. First Drug Administration
    C. Food and Drug Administration
    D. Finding Drug Allergies

6. Which type of food is **not** mentioned?
    A. fruit
    B. seafood
    C. meat
    D. nuts

INFERENCE

7. What is the disagreement over GE foods?
    A. GE foods don't look normal.
    B. People can't agree on their safety.
    C. They are better than natural foods.
    D. GE foods are less nutritious.

8. What is true about GE foods?
    A. GE foods may cause allergic reactions.
    B. Supporters of GE foods say they are dangerous.
    C. GE foods aren't altered in any way.
    D. There are no groups concerned about GE foods.

VOCABULARY REVIEW

CROSSWORD PUZZLE

Complete the crossword using the clues.

ACROSS

4. If something is one of a kind, it is _____.

5. Something that all people do around the world is _____.

6. If someone makes you feel you can do something, he/she _____ you.

7. Ingredients and instructions for a food.

8. The type of code in genes.

DOWN

1. Cheerful.

2. A work of great skill.

3. Kind and giving.

WRONG WORD

One word in each group does not fit. Circle the word.

1. chocolate   recipe   cookbook   proverb

2. spa   gourmet   treatment   massage

3. masterpiece   attraction   zoo   museum

4. generous   kind   beautiful   giving

5. nutrition   virus   diet   meal

6. unique   unusual   different   genetic

Fill in the blanks with words from each box.

| accomplish | alter | individually | proverb | resist |

1. I love chocolate. Every time someone offers me some I can't _____ .
2. Education is very important. It helps people _____ their dreams.
3. A _____ is a special saying that is passed down from generation to generation.
4. Many chefs _____ traditional recipes to create new dishes.
5. To keep my home-baked cookies fresh, I wrap them _____ .

| allergic | gourmet | legacy | opponents | souvenir |

6. Julia Child loved to entertain friends with _____ meals.
7. I have a beautiful model of the Eiffel Tower. I bought it as a _____ in Paris.
8. I can't eat nuts or seafood. I'm _____ to them.
9. My mother was an amazing person. Her honesty and big heart were her _____ .
10. _____ of the new night club said that they didn't like the loud music late at night.

| community | development | generous | exquisite | unimaginable |

11. Did you hear about the newest _____ in genetic engineering?
12. Pablo Picasso created _____ pieces of art.
13. I never expected him to behave so badly. What he did was _____ .
14. Most people prefer to raise kids in a quiet, friendly _____ .
15. Mother Teresa was a _____ person. She dedicated her life to helping those in need.

Fill in the blanks with words from each box.

| inspire *(verb)* | inspiration *(noun)* | inspirational *(adjective)* |

1. Great teachers are able to _____ their students.
2. Stories with happy endings are _____ . They give people hope.

imagine *(verb)*	imagination *(noun)*	unimaginable *(adjective)*

3. George Lucas, the creator of *Star Wars,* has a great _____ .

4. Can you _____ the world without chocolate?

resist *(verb)*	resistance *(noun)*	resistant *(adjective)*

5. Doctors worry about diseases that have become _____ to modern drugs.

6. Who can _____ a gourmet meal?

WRAP IT UP

DISCUSS THE THEME

Read these questions and discuss them with your partner.

1. Do you think you eat the right foods? Explain your answer and give some examples of nutritious meals.

2. Are you a good cook? If so, who taught you to cook?

3. What was the first thing you cooked?

4. Do you like to invite friends and family over to eat? What types of food do you serve?

5. Describe a place that has unique foods. What is unique about it?

RESPOND IN WRITING

Look back at the unit and choose the passage you enjoyed the most. Read it again. Write a short summary of the passage.

_____

_____

_____

_____

_____

What do you think is the most interesting thing about this passage, and why? Write a short paragraph.

_____

_____

_____

_____

_____

_____

ARCHITECTURE
MODERN BUILDINGS

Construction of the Chicago Twin Towers, 1950

BEFORE YOU READ

Answer these questions.

1. What are your favorite buildings?

2. What do you like about them?

3. What are some examples of modern architecture?

CHAPTER 1

Mies van der Rohe,
1886–1969

Discuss these questions.

1. Imagine your dream house. What does it look like?

2. What qualities or skills should a good architect have?

WORD FOCUS

Match the words with their definitions.

A.

1. admire ___   **a.** a very tall building with many floors
2. architect ___   **b.** able to be easily changed
3. design ___   **c.** like someone or something very much
4. flexible ___   **d.** a person who designs buildings
5. high-rise ___   **e.** make a plan for a building

B.

1. influence ___   **a.** a tall narrow building or part of a building
2. partition ___   **b.** a person who cuts or builds with stones
3. skyscraper ___   **c.** a wall used to divide a space into parts
4. stonemason ___   **d.** have an effect on someone's actions or thoughts
5. tower ___   **e.** a very tall building with many floors

SCAN

Guess if this is true or false. Circle *a* or *b*.

Ludwig Mies van der Rohe was born in New York.

a. True   **b.** False

Scan the passage quickly to check your answer.

Mies van der Rohe: Modern Architect

Ludwig Mies van der Rohe was one of the most famous **architects** of the 20th century. He **designed** some of the world's first **skyscrapers**. People
5 still **admire** his buildings because they are simple and flexible. People may not know his name, but they have heard his favorite saying: "Less is more."

Mies was born in Germany in 1886.
10 He was the son of a **stonemason**, and this is how he learned about buildings. Mies studied with some of the most famous architects in Germany in the years before World War I.

15 After the war, Mies studied the skyscraper. He drew designs for two tall steel **towers** with walls of glass. These towers were never built, but other architects admired his work. His ideas
20 for building skyscrapers with glass walls became well known. He **influenced** the design of skyscrapers in the 1940s and 1950s. This style of design was called the "International Style." The buildings were
25 simple, rectangular, and mostly glass. Examples include Corning Glass Works in New York state, New York City's United Nations Building, and the BC Electric Building in Vancouver, Canada.

30 However, few of the skyscrapers that Mies designed were built. As a result, he began to design smaller buildings. He was among the first to design modern apartments, homes, and even a large
35 convention center.

In 1927, Mies designed a building for an international fair in Barcelona, Spain. This building had a flat roof and no columns for support. The inside walls
40 were made of glass and marble. The walls could be moved around because they did not support the roof. These inner walls are called partitions, and they are often used in convention centers
45 today. Simple and flexible spaces like this are typical of all of his designs.

In 1937, Mies moved to Chicago. He soon started work on one of his most famous buildings, the Farnsworth house.
50 This was a weekend vacation "dream home" in the countryside outside of Chicago. The house was a single room with partitions, and the outside walls were glass. Throughout the 1950s Mies
55 continued to design buildings with open and flexible spaces.

Finally, one of his skyscrapers was built. In 1951, the Chicago Twin Towers were completed. In the next three years,
60 other high-rises designed by Mies were built in New York, Detroit, and Toronto. When the Seagram Building was finished in New York in 1954, it was called a masterpiece of skyscraper design.

65 In 1962, Mies designed a new national art gallery in Berlin. This building has the same feeling of his other buildings. The walls are made of glass, the roof is low and flat, and the inside
70 space has movable partitions. Mies visited the building many times during construction. Unfortunately, he died in Chicago on August 17, 1969 before the museum opened.

75 His ideas did not die with him, and Ludwig Mies van der Rohe will always be famous for his simple and flexible designs. And people will also remember his words: "Less is more."

Read the passage again and answer the questions. Circle your answers.

MAIN IDEA

1. What is the main topic of the passage?
   A. a builder
   B. an architect
   C. skyscapers
   D. apartments and houses

DETAIL

2. What is the name of Mies's style of design?
   A. German Style
   B. Chicago Style
   C. New York Style
   D. International Style

3. What did Mies design in Berlin?
   A. a skyscraper
   B. an apartment block
   C. a convention center
   D. an art gallery

4. When was Mies's first skyscraper built?
   A. 1927
   B. 1937
   C. 1951
   D. 1954

5. Why did Mies begin to design smaller buildings?
   A. They were more beautiful than bigger buildings.
   B. He moved to the U.S.
   C. Few of his skyscraper designs were built.
   D. They had no partitions.

6. Which of these materials was most important in his designs?
   A. glass
   B. wood
   C. concrete
   D. stone

INFERENCE

7. What do you think Mies meant when he said "Less is more"?
   A. Bigger is better.
   B. Simple is better.
   C. Taller is better.
   D. More rooms are better.

8. Which of the following statements is true?
   A. Mies built skyscrapers and smaller buildings.
   B. Mies was an influential designer.
   C. Mies liked to design with glass.
   D. all of the above

CHAPTER 2

◀ The Farnsworth House

PREPARE TO READ

Discuss these questions.

1. Describe the house in the photo.

2. Would you enjoy living in a glass house? Why or why not?

WORD FOCUS

Match the words with their definitions.

A.
1. client ___
2. closet ___
3. condense ___
4. enemy ___
5. function ___

a. a person who dislikes another person very much
b. a specific purpose
c. a small place with a door for storing clothes
d. customer; a person who receives a service
e. when water changes from a gas to a liquid

B.
1. harmony ___
2. install ___
3. physician ___
4. screen ___
5. slab ___

a. put a piece of equipment in place
b. a wire or plastic net on a window that allows air to pass but not insects
c. a state of agreement of feelings
d. a large flat piece of something
e. medical doctor

SCAN

Guess if this is true or false. Circle *a* or *b*.

Edith Farnsworth was a doctor.

a. True   **b.** False

Scan the passage quickly to check your answer.

The Farnsworth House

Mies van der Rohe believed that a home could be more than just a place to live. He believed that a home could be a work of art. In 1946 he presented this
5 idea to Dr. Edith Farnsworth, a wealthy Chicago **physician**, when she asked him to design a weekend home outside of the city.

Mies and Farnsworth were good
10 friends. When the house was finished five years later, they were **enemies**. The architect and the **client** argued over form and **function**. Farnsworth was unhappy with both the house and
15 the cost. The house cost $73,000. That equals half-a-million dollars in today's money.

From a distance the Farnsworth house looks like a rectangular glass box.
20 The house is a single open room with glass walls. Like a skyscraper, simple steel columns support the house. The roof and the floor are flat concrete **slabs**. The house is near a river, and Mies was
25 worried about flooding. To help protect the house from floods, he built the house five feet above the ground. With clear glass walls from floor to ceiling on all sides, the house seems to float above the
30 ground.

Mies tried to build a house in **harmony** with nature. In cold weather the house is heated by special coils in the concrete floor. In hot weather the
35 house is cooled by opening the doors and windows. This allows air to circulate through the only room.

Glass houses like this one have many problems. Because of all the glass,
40 Farnsworth's heating bills were very high in winter. Also, water **condenses** on the cold surface of the windows and forms drops. In summer, the glass allows sunlight in, which heats up the room.
45 Mies did not **install** air conditioning, and he did not put in **screens** to keep insects out. On hot summer nights, the lights from inside attracted thousands of mosquitoes. Farnsworth was also
50 upset that there were no **closets** in the house. Mies told her that since it was a weekend house, she only needed to bring one dress!

Farnsworth called the house unlivable.
55 Mies said it was a work of art. Mies would not let Farnsworth's complaints disturb his design.

Some say the Farnsworth house seems more like a simple Japanese temple than
60 a home. The glass walls make it seem like one is living outdoors surrounded by nature. Other people find the house bare and lifeless. Dr. Farnsworth once said, "We know that less is not more. It
65 is simply less!"

Dr. Farnsworth hated her new weekend home. In 1971, she finally sold it to a man who collects houses. The buyer knew that the house was a work
70 of art. The new owner placed large fans in each corner of the room to keep the house cool in summer. On hot summer days he kept the doors and windows open. He lived there and did not
75 complain about the insects. However, he only stayed in the house a few weeks each year.

Mies built a house that is in harmony with nature, but no one lives there
80 anymore. Today the house stays open as a museum and a work of art.

Read the passage again and answer the questions. Circle your answers.

MAIN IDEA

1. What is the main topic of the passage?
   A. how to choose an architect
   B. problems between an architect and client
   C. a house collector
   D. homes of rich and famous people

DETAIL

2. Which of these statements describes Mies's feelings about a house?
   A. It should be comfortable.
   B. It should be a work of art.
   C. It should have few windows.
   D. It should be easy to heat and cool.

3. When did Mies finish the house?
   A. 1946
   B. 1951
   C. 1971
   D. 1996

4. Why did Mies build the house above the ground?
   A. He wanted it to float.
   B. He was worried about floods.
   C. He wanted harmony with nature.
   D. He wanted to keep insects outside.

5. Which of the following was a problem with the house?
   A. It was difficult to heat.
   B. It had no water.
   C. There were too many rooms.
   D. The windows did not open.

6. What can you use to keep insects out?
   A. air conditioning
   B. concrete slabs
   C. special coils
   D. screens

INFERENCE

7. Why did Farnsworth sell the house?
   A. She didn't like it.
   B. It didn't have enough closets.
   C. She hated the insects.
   D. all of the above

8. Which of these statements describes the house collector?
   A. He hated the house and tore it down.
   B. He loved the house so much that he lived in it all year.
   C. He sold the house back to Mies.
   D. He did not agree with Dr. Farnsworth about the house.

CHAPTER 3

◀ Jin Mao Tower, Shanghai

PREPARE TO READ

Discuss these questions.

1. What is the tallest building in the world? Where is it?
2. Have you ever seen or been up one of the world's tallest buildings?

WORD FOCUS

Match the words with their definitions.

A.

1. claim ___   **a.** how tall something is
2. compete ___   **b.** move forward
3. height ___   **c.** try to be better than somebody else
4. pride ___   **d.** the positive feeling you have about the place you live
5. progress ___   **e.** say something is yours because you are first or best

B.

1. rest ___   **a.** social or professional position in relation to other people
2. spire ___   **b.** all the remaining things in a group
3. status ___   **c.** a tall pointed tower on the top of a building
4. symbol ___   **d.** for a short time
5. temporarily ___ **e.** a sign or an object that represents an idea

SCAN

Guess if this is true or false. Circle *a* or *b*.

The tallest buildings in the world are in the United States.

a. True   **b.** False

Scan the passage quickly to check your answer.

Skyscrapers

Tall, taller, tallest. For much of the 20th century, New York City and Chicago **competed** to build the world's tallest skyscrapers. Other cities around
5 the world watched the race between these two cities. From 1913 to 1930 New York's Woolworth Building was the tallest (792 ft/241 m). From 1931 until 1972, the Empire State Building in
10 New York was the tallest building in the world (1,250 ft/381 m). Then Chicago built its own Sears Tower, which stood as the tallest building in the world (1,450 ft/442 m) for 24 years. Until the
15 1990s, the United States **claimed** the tallest structures on earth. That is no longer true. Today the tallest buildings are in Asia.

The economies of Asia are growing.
20 Skyscrapers are a **symbol** of this growth. Fifteen years ago, nine of the world's 10 tallest buildings were in the United States. Now there are just two: the Sears Tower in Chicago and the Empire State
25 Building in New York. The **rest** are in Asia. The tall building is the new **status** symbol, just as it once was for New York and Chicago.

Skyscrapers were originally built by
30 wealthy companies as symbols of their success and power. That is still true today. But skyscrapers are also symbols of local and national **pride**. Countries compete to build the tallest structure.
35 Since 1998, the race to be the tallest has **progressed** quickly. Petronas Twin Towers was completed in Kuala, Lumpur in 1997 (1,483 ft/452 m). Just one year later, Shanghai completed
40 the Jin Mao Tower (1,381 ft/421 m). Shanghai plans to add the even taller

World Finance Center (1,614 ft/492 m). In 2004, Taipei 101 was completed (1,671 ft/509 m). And now Dubai in the
45 Middle East has entered the race. This small country has plans to complete an even taller skyscraper. Everyone involved is keeping the final **height** of the Dubai building a secret. They don't
50 want another country to build a bigger skyscraper before theirs is finished.

The newer skyscrapers don't look anything like the towering glass-walled buildings of mid-20th century America.
55 Asian countries have rejected plain glass and steel boxes as a Western import. The new skyscrapers in Asia have their own new unique styles. Petronas Towers reminds people of a mosque rising
60 high above the city. Jin Mao Tower in Shanghai looks like a very high, very long pagoda.

Skyscrapers demand to be noticed. They are a source of local and national
65 pride. Cities ask how they can make existing buildings even taller. As an example, the Petronas Towers were originally designed without **spires**. The finished building would not have been
70 tall enough to beat the Sears Tower in Chicago, so the builder of the tower asked the designers to add spires. The spires made the building 20 feet (6 m) higher, and that was enough to make
75 their building the tallest in the world, at least **temporarily**.

Yesterday it was America. Today, Asia. Tomorrow, Dubai. And Dubai is keeping its secret about how high its building is
80 going to be.

Read the passage again and answer the questions. Circle your answers.

MAIN IDEA

1. What is the main topic of the passage?
   A. designing skyscrapers
   B. competing to build the tallest skyscrapers
   C. comparing American and Asian cities
   D. finding jobs for architects

DETAIL

2. In 1920, the world's tallest building was the
   A. Empire State Building
   B. Woolworth Building
   C. Sears Tower
   D. Petronas Twin Towers

3. How tall is Jin Mao Tower?
   A. 1,381 feet (421 m)
   B. 1,450 feet (442 m)
   C. 1,483 feet (452 m)
   D. 1,614 feet (492 m)

4. Which building is the tallest?
   A. Sears Tower
   B. Petronas Twin Towers
   C. Taipei 101
   D. Jin Mao Tower

5. Why is the word *race* used in this passage?
   A. It describes the competition between countries.
   B. The workers run to work every morning.
   C. It describes different people.
   D. One building is owned by a car company.

6. What do the new skyscrapers look like?
   A. glass boxes
   B. steel towers
   C. plain and simple
   D. none of the above

INFERENCE

7. Why are Asian cities building skyscrapers?
   A. Skyscrapers are a source of pride.
   B. Asian cities can afford to build skyscrapers.
   C. They want to have the tallest buildings.
   D. all of the above

8. Which of these statements is true about spires?
   A. They are extra floors added to a building.
   B. They are added to make a building seem smaller.
   C. They are more expensive than extra floors.
   D. They are sometimes just for decoration.

VOCABULARY REVIEW

CROSSWORD PUZZLE

Complete the crossword using the clues.

ACROSS

1. A place to store clothes.

3. This is used to keep insects out.

4. The opposite of *friend*.

5. A tall structure.

7. Put equipment in place.

DOWN

1. A customer is also a _____.

2. How tall something is.

3. A sign or an object that represents an idea.

6. The others from the group.

WRONG WORD

One word in each group does not fit. Circle the word.

1. high-rise	skyscraper	stonemason	tower
2. architect	designer	physician	engineer
3. agreement	spire	contract	document
4. admire	like	friend	enemy
5. partition	influence	closet	wall
6. condense	compete	race	game

Fill in the blanks with words from each box.

flexible	influenced	high-rise	partition	pride

1. The client bought an apartment in the new _____.

2. I want to be able to change my living space. I want my home to be _____.

3. This is a great place to live. We all take great _____ in our city.

4. Who _____ you to study architecture? Was it your father?

5. You will need to put up a _____ to divide the room into more private spaces.

client	condensed	enemies	harmony	progressed

6. Water _____ on the glass in the bathroom.

7. The _____ asked for a lot of changes to the design.

8. At first they were good friends, but later they became _____.

9. Work on the new building has _____ quickly.

10. He believed in living in _____ with nature.

closet	compete	screen	spires	symbol

11. You need to _____ against others in order to win the prize.

12. A _____ in the window will keep insects out of the house.

13. Each of the bedrooms has a big _____. There is plenty of room for clothes.

14. The architect decided to add two _____ to the top of the skyscraper.

15. Many people think that expensive cars and homes are a _____ of power.

WORD FAMILIES

Fill in the blanks with words from each box.

admire *(verb)*	admiration *(noun)*	admirable *(adjective)*

1. I _____ my friend. She never gets bad grades in school.

2. Her performance on the last exam was _____. She got 100%.

| function *(verb)* | function *(noun)* | functional *(adjective)* |

3. Cars _____ best when you check gas and oil regularly.

4. I prefer to buy furniture that is cheap and _____ .

| install *(verb)* | installation *(noun)* | installer *(noun)* |

5. We have to _____ new glass in the window.

6. The _____ probably won't be too difficult.

WRAP IT UP

DISCUSS THE THEME

Read these questions and discuss them with your partner.

1. What is the tallest building you have been in?
  - Did you go to the top of the building?
  - How long did it take to get up to the top?
  - How did you get to the top—on an elevator or by stairs? How did you get down?
  - What was at the top?
  - How did it feel to be that high up?
  - Were you able to see out at the top? What could you see?

2. What are some of the advantages of very tall buildings? What are some of the disadvantages?

RESPOND IN WRITING

Look back at the unit and choose the passage you enjoyed the most. Read it again. Write a short summary of the passage.

_____

_____

_____

_____

_____

What do you think is the most interesting thing about this passage, and why? Write a short paragraph.

_____

_____

_____

_____

_____

_____

AFRICAN AMERICAN STUDIES

MUSIC

Marian Anderson singing at the
Lincoln Memorial

BEFORE YOU READ

Answer these questions.

1. Who is your favorite singer?

2. What is that singer's style of music?

3. Have you ever heard that singer perform in concert?

CHAPTER 1

Marian Anderson, 1897–1993
(portrait by Laura Wheeler
Waring, 1944)

PREPARE TO READ

Discuss these questions.

1. Do you ever listen to opera music?

2. How do opera singers learn to sing so well?

WORD FOCUS

Match the words with their definitions.

A.

1. choir ___   **a.** a statement that says something nice about someone
2. competition ___   **b.** a group of people who sing together
3. compliment ___   **c.** the person who directs the musicians in an orchestra
4. conductor ___   **d.** the ability to control fear in a dangerous or unpleasant situation
5. courage ___   **e.** an event in which people try to win something

B.

1. inauguration ___   **a.** playing, singing, or dancing in front of an audience
2. inequality ___   **b.** keeping one group separate from another because of race
3. performance ___   **c.** a natural skill or ability
4. segregation ___   **d.** a special ceremony for a new official or leader
5. talent ___   **e.** a difference between groups because one has more advantages

SCAN

Guess if this is true or false. Circle *a* or *b*.

Marian Anderson sang at the inauguration of President Roosevelt.

a. True   **b.** False

Scan the passage quickly to check your answer.

Marian Anderson: A Singer's Journey

Marian Anderson was an African American and one of the world's greatest singers. She lived during a time of **inequality** for African Americans in the United States. Marian Anderson's **talent** and **courage** opened doors for men and women of color.

Anderson was born in Philadelphia, Pennsylvania in 1897. Anderson's father died when she was ten, and her family had little money. She always loved music and singing. As a child, she sang in her church **choir**. Everyone admired her voice, and many people told her to take lessons. Her mother could not afford singing lessons, so members of her church raised money for lessons.

Anderson had a strong voice. She was able to sing both operas and popular music. She took lessons from several talented singers of the time. In 1925, she won an important **competition**. The prize was a chance to sing with the New York Philharmonic Orchestra. Her **performance** was very successful, but she had trouble finding work in the United States. Because she was African American, she was not allowed to perform in many theaters.

Anderson decided to move to Europe. There she sang in many famous opera houses. When she performed in Austria, the famous **conductor** Arturo Toscanini heard her. He said, "A voice like yours is heard only once in a hundred years." This was a great **compliment** from such a famous artist.

Anderson returned to the United States in 1935. She sang at Town Hall in New York City in 1936. The next year, she sang at the White House. She was a well-known singer, and many people wanted to hear her. However, in 1939, Anderson had a problem that became big news. She was not permitted to sing at Constitution Hall in Washington, D.C. Because of **segregation**, the owners of the hall only allowed white artists to perform there. This angered many people, including Eleanor Roosevelt, the wife of the president.

Eleanor Roosevelt believed that segregation was wrong, so she invited Anderson to sing on the steps of the Lincoln Memorial. More than 75,000 people came to hear Anderson sing. Millions of people heard her on the radio. They heard her beautiful voice and realized that her color had nothing to do with her singing ability. This performance was important for all Americans. More and more people questioned the segregation laws of the time.

Anderson opened doors for many African American performers. In 1955, she sang at the Metropolitan Opera House in New York City. She was the first African American to sing there. In 1957, Anderson sang on a tour of several East Asian countries. This tour was for the United Nations. In 1963, she sang at the **inauguration** of President John F. Kennedy. Millions of people watched on television or listened to the radio as she sang for the president.

Marian Anderson died in 1993 at age 98. She saw many changes during her lifetime, and she helped change the lives of many people. She showed that ability is more important than skin color.

Read the passage again and answer the questions. Circle your answers.

MAIN IDEA

1. What is the main topic of the passage?
   A. a famous singer's career in Europe
   B. how Eleanor Roosevelt changed history
   C. the importance of singing lessons
   D. a famous African American singer

DETAIL

2. When Anderson was a child, she sang in
   A. New York
   B. a church choir
   C. a school choir
   D. Austria

3. Why did the members of Anderson's church raise money for singing lessons?
   A. They liked to raise money.
   B. Anderson's voice was bad, so she needed lessons.
   C. Anderson's mother couldn't afford lessons.
   D. They raised money every year for someone in the church.

4. Where did the conductor Arturo Toscanini hear Anderson sing?
   A. in Italy
   B. at President Kennedy's inauguration
   C. at the Lincoln Memorial
   D. in Austria

5. Where did Marian Anderson sing?
   A. Town Hall in New York City
   B. the White House in Washington, D.C.
   C. Metropolitan Opera House in New York City
   D. all of the above

6. Eleanor Roosevelt thought that
   A. Marian Anderson needed singing lessons
   B. segregation was wrong
   C. Marian Anderson sang in a choir
   D. Marian Anderson should move to Europe

INFERENCE

7. Anderson was **not** allowed to sing at Constitution Hall because
   A. she wasn't a U.S. citizen
   B. she was a woman
   C. she was African American
   D. she was too young

8. In what way did radio and television help Anderson?
   A. They allowed more people to hear her.
   B. They showed that women could sing as well as men.
   C. They showed that her European training was important.
   D. They proved that she was popular.

CHAPTER 2

The Lincoln Memorial

PREPARE TO READ

Discuss these questions.

1. Which city is the Lincoln Memorial in?

2. What important things happened at this location?

WORD FOCUS

Match the words with their definitions.

A.

1. assassinate ___
2. broadcast ___
3. free ___
4. honor ___
5. historic ___

a. show great public respect for someone or something
b. not controlled by other people
c. famous or important to remember
d. kill an important person, often for political reasons
e. something that is sent out by radio or on television

B.

1. massive ___
2. monument ___
3. shallow ___
4. slavery ___
5. statue ___

a. something built to remind people of an important person or event
b. the owning of another person
c. a figure of a person or an animal usually in a public place
d. not deep
e. very large

SCAN

Guess if this is true or false. Circle *a* or *b*.

There is a statue of Lincoln inside the Lincoln Memorial.

a. True   **b.** False

Scan the passage quickly to check your answer.

The Lincoln Memorial

Many important events have taken place at the Lincoln Memorial in Washington, D.C. This beautiful **monument** was built to **honor** Abraham
5 Lincoln, the sixteenth president of the United States. Abraham Lincoln is one of the nation's most honored presidents.

Abraham Lincoln was president during the U.S. Civil War in the 1860s.
10 In this long, terrible war, the North fought against the South. Brother fought against brother. The major cause of this war was **slavery**. President Lincoln felt that all people should
15 be **free**. The Southern states wanted slavery to continue. The Southern states left the union and formed their own government. The Northern states fought to keep the country together.
20 After several years of fighting, the North won the war and the slaves won their freedom. Not long after the Civil War ended, Lincoln was **assassinated**.

Lincoln and the monument to honor
25 him are symbols of the fight for freedom. The memorial has a long, **shallow** pool in front. It has tall columns and **massive** steps that lead to a large **statue** of the president. The statue of Lincoln
30 sits facing toward the pool. This pool is called a reflecting pool because its water is like a mirror. The monument to another great president is directly across in the distance: the Washington
35 Monument. The two monuments face each other across the long reflecting pool. The tall spire of the Washington Monument is reflected in the pool. An open grassy area next to the reflecting
40 pool provides space for many people to gather.

The steps of the Lincoln Memorial have been the site of several important events in U.S. history. The great Marian
45 Anderson sang on the steps of the Lincoln Memorial in 1939. First Lady Eleanor Roosevelt invited Anderson to sing there. Anderson's performance became a symbol of the fight against
50 segregation. Anderson sang on the steps of the memorial to the president who fought for freedom. Her concert was in the open air, and it was free. Everyone was allowed to attend. There
55 was no charge to listen to her music in this public place. About 75,000 people attended. A radio **broadcast** of the performance allowed millions of Americans to hear Anderson sing about
60 freedom.

The Lincoln Memorial is a place where many have come to speak of freedom. In 1963, Dr. Martin Luther King gave a **historic** speech called, "I
65 Have a Dream." In this famous speech, he called for freedom for every person in the United States. Many thousands of people listened on the steps of the memorial and in the grassy area as Dr.
70 King gave his speech. This speech was important in the fight for civil rights. Dr. King inspired many people to fight for freedom and for the rights of all citizens. In 1968, like Lincoln, he too
75 was assassinated.

By choosing this location, both Anderson and King honored Lincoln, the man who believed in freedom for all people. The Lincoln Memorial remains a
80 symbol of the fight for freedom.

Read the passage again and answer the questions. Circle your answers.

MAIN IDEA

1. What is the main topic of the passage?
   A. places where people sing in Washington, D.C.
   B. a memorial that represents freedom
   C. important events at the Washington Monument
   D. how the Lincoln Memorial was built

DETAIL

2. When was Lincoln killed?
   A. before the Civil War
   B. in the second year of the Civil War
   C. in the fourth year of the Civil War
   D. after the Civil War

3. Which of these things does the Lincoln Memorial include?
   A. a statue, columns, and steps
   B. a tall spire and a statue
   C. a deep pool inside
   D. all of the above

4. Which of these people gave speeches at the Lincoln Memorial?
   A. Marian Anderson
   B. Martin Luther King
   C. Abraham Lincoln
   D. all of the above

5. President Lincoln believed that
   A. all people should be free
   B. brothers should fight brothers
   C. the South should have its own government
   D. some people should be slaves

6. Dr. King's speech was important because
   A. he was assassinated
   B. he liked Marian Anderson's music
   C. he knew Lincoln
   D. he inspired people to fight for their rights

INFERENCE

7. The Lincoln Memorial and the Washington Monument
   A. are both important symbols
   B. are relatively small monuments
   C. were both built before the Civil War
   D. are similar to each other

8. Which of the following statements is true?
   A. Anderson and King both met Abraham Lincoln.
   B. Marian Anderson fought to free the slaves.
   C. Lincoln and King were both killed because of their beliefs.
   D. People must pay a fee to speak near the reflecting pool.

CHAPTER 3

◀ Louis Armstrong, 1900–1971

PREPARE TO READ

Discuss these questions.

1. Have you ever listened to jazz or gospel music?

2. Where did you hear this type of music?

WORD FOCUS

Match the words with their definitions.

A.

1. clap ___   **a.** a style of religious music popular with African Americans
2. festival ___   **b.** put your hands together quickly to make a loud sound
3. gospel ___   **c.** a building or large room where concerts or classes are held
4. hall ___   **d.** a song that people sing in church
5. hymn ___   **e.** a large public celebration held regularly in one place

B.

1. influence ___   **a.** an area where ships load or unload goods and passengers
2. lively ___   **b.** in a place near you
3. local ___   **c.** a regular repeated pattern of sound
4. port ___   **d.** full of energy
5. rhythm ___   **e.** something that affects or changes something else

SCAN

Guess if this is true or false. Circle *a* or *b*.

The Beatles listened to jazz.

a. True   **b.** False

Scan the passage quickly to check your answer.

Jazz and Gospel Music

The **rhythms** of African music arrived in the United States with the African slaves. This music was the basis for later African American musical developments.
African Americans in the 19th and 20th century created several new styles of music. Two of these are jazz and **gospel** music. These unique styles of music are popular around the world.

Jazz was born around 1895 in New Orleans, Louisiana. Jazz developed from work songs, **hymns**, and gospel music. At first, only African American musicians played jazz. Soon other musicians heard the unique sounds of jazz and began to perform this style of music.

New Orleans was the early center of jazz in the United States. New Orleans is a southern **port** city. People from many cultures come together there. There is a large African American community, and there are also **influences** from Mexico and the Caribbean.

There were many jazz **halls** in New Orleans at the beginning of the 20th century. In the 1920s, African American musicians from New Orleans moved north to Chicago. In Chicago, the musicians had more freedom, and their music was heard by more people. Chicago became the new center of jazz. It was in Chicago that jazz was first recorded. Jazz wasn't just a **local** music form anymore. It became popular with everyone. Jazz also influenced white musicians. The Beatles, a famous British group in the 1960s and 1970s, listened to jazz musicians and tried to copy their rhythms.

African Americans also created gospel music. Gospel is a type of religious music. During slavery, African Americans weren't allowed to practice their own religions. Slaves had to practice the religion of their owners. Slaves also had to sing the hymns of their owners. Over time, African American singers changed the hymns. The singers added new ideas and emotions. Some gospel music talks of troubles and problems. It tells people not to give up. During slavery, some gospel music urged slaves to go north to find freedom.

When Marian Anderson performed at the Lincoln Memorial in 1939, she sang the song, "Nobody Knows the Trouble I've Seen." This very emotional song speaks of the difficulties that African Americans faced. Some of the words are:

Sometimes I'm up and sometimes
  I'm down
Yes, lord, you know sometimes
  I'm almost to the ground

This sad song speaks of struggles and of overcoming problems. People understood the feelings expressed in this song. Many people had these same problems and felt these same emotions.

Other gospel music is very **lively**. The energetic rhythm encourages people to **clap** their hands and move their feet. It lets people forget about their troubles. Large choirs of singers often perform gospel music.

Today there are many jazz **festivals** in the United States, and gospel music is no longer heard only in churches. Choirs sing the beautiful gospel music at many ceremonies and events. What began as two local forms of African American music has spread all over the world.

Read the passage again and answer the questions. Circle your answers.

MAIN IDEA

1. What is the main topic of the passage?
   A. two famous cities
   B. two famous gospel singers
   C. two African American musical styles
   D. two centuries of music

DETAIL

2. Jazz began
   A. in New York in 1895
   B. in New Orleans in 1895
   C. in Chicago in 1920
   D. in England in 1920

3. What happened in Chicago?
   A. Jazz was born.
   B. Jazz musicians had less freedom.
   C. The first jazz recording was made.
   D. The Beatles first played jazz.

4. Which of the following statements is true?
   A. African music was the basis for jazz and gospel music.
   B. African American slaves had freedom of religion.
   C. All gospel songs are slow and sad.
   D. Jazz had little influence on other musicians.

5. The rhythm of gospel music makes people
   A. clap their hands
   B. move their feet
   C. forget their troubles
   D. all of the above

6. Today jazz and gospel music are
   A. heard all over the world
   B. never heard at festivals
   C. only heard in churches
   D. only played by African Americans

INFERENCE

7. Jazz started in New Orleans because
   A. many African American musicians lived there
   B. the city had no other type of music
   C. musicians like to play music on ships
   D. it was difficult for musicians to find work there

8. The song that Marian Anderson sang
   A. was a famous song by the Beatles
   B. urged people to move to the North
   C. made people clap their hands and move their feet
   D. caused people to feel strong emotions

VOCABULARY REVIEW

CROSSWORD PUZZLE

Complete the crossword using the clues.

ACROSS

1. Famous or important.
4. You do this with your hands.
5. Ships sail into a _____.
6. Not deep.

DOWN

1. Show great public respect.
2. Natural skill or ability.
3. The control of fear is _____.
6. A figure in a public place.

WRONG WORD

One word in each group does not fit. Circle the word.

1. inequality   slavery   segregation   choir
2. perform   sing   play   free
3. massive   lively   huge   large
4. struggle   problem   honor   difficulty
5. festival   party   celebration   rhythm
6. radio   statue   broadcast   television

Fill in the blanks with words from each box.

compliment	inauguration	monument	performance	shallow

1. Anderson received a _____ from a great artist.

2. The water in the pool is quite _____. It is only a few inches deep.

3. Anderson's _____ at the Lincoln Memorial was very successful.

4. The _____ honors the men and women who fought for freedom.

5. Anderson sang at President Kennedy's _____ in Washington, D.C.

inspired	local	rhythm	slaves	statue

6. We danced to the _____ of the music.

7. The songs about freedom _____ many people.

8. At 5:00, we listened to the _____ news on television.

9. _____ were people who were not free.

10. There is a _____ of Lincoln inside his memorial.

broadcast	clap	influenced	ports	talent

11. Sometimes people _____ their hands in time to the music.

12. He was a man of great _____. His voice was known everywhere.

13. Many cultures have _____ jazz.

14. New York and Miami are both busy _____.

15. Millions of people heard the radio _____.

WORD FAMILIES

Fill in the blanks with words from each box.

performer (noun)	performance (noun)	perform (verb)

1. Many musicians wanted to _____ in Constitution Hall.

2. The singer's _____ was a great success.

| free *(adjective)* | free *(verb)* | freedom *(noun)* |

3. The Civil War was fought to _____ the slaves.

4. The song was about _____ and courage.

| honor *(noun)* | honor *(verb)* | honorable *(adjective)* |

5. She did the _____ thing. She apologized.

6. The city is going to _____ him with a monument.

WRAP IT UP

DISCUSS THE THEME

Read these questions and discuss them with your partner.

1. Have you ever gone to a concert?

2. Describe the experience.
   • What type of music was it? Who performed?
   • Where was the performance? When was it?
   • How did the audience react?
   • Was the performance for some special event?
   • Did you enjoy the performance? Why or why not?

3. How is a live concert different from a recording? Which do you prefer?

RESPOND IN WRITING

Look back at the unit and choose the passage you enjoyed the most. Read it again. Write a short summary of the passage.

_____

_____

_____

_____

_____

_____

**What do you think is the most interesting thing about this passage, and why?
Write a short paragraph.**

_____

_____

_____

_____

_____

_____

U.S. HISTORY
EXPLORATION

The explorer Coronado in his search for gold

BEFORE YOU READ

Answer these questions.

1. Look at the image above. Describe what you see.

2. Can you name any other explorers? Where did they go?

3. Do explorers always find what they are looking for?

CHAPTER 1

Francisco de Coronado, 1510–1544

PREPARE TO READ

Discuss these questions.

1. Have you ever visited another country? Where did you go?
2. Was it as you expected it to be? In what ways was it different?

WORD FOCUS

Match the words with their definitions.

A.
1. adventure ___   **a.** take someone prisoner
2. assistant ___   **b.** add something in order to make a thing more attractive
3. capture ___   **c.** a person who helps someone else
4. charge ___   **d.** an experience or event that is very unusual, exciting, or dangerous
5. decorate ___   **e.** an official claim that someone has done something against the law

B.
1. explorer ___   **a.** a long search
2. legendary ___   **b.** very valuable objects such as gold or jewels
3. quest ___   **c.** from an old story that may or may not be true
4. treasure ___   **d.** a person searching for treasure
5. treasure hunter ___   **e.** a person who travels around to find out about a place

SCAN

Guess if this is true or false. Circle a or b.

Coronado found gold in the American Southwest.

a. True   **b.** False

Scan the passage quickly to check your answer.

Francisco de Coronado: Explorer

The early Spanish **explorers** came to the New World in the 1500s in search of gold. Francisco de Coronado was one of these explorers. The story of Coronado
5 is one of riches and **adventure**. In his **quest** for gold, Francisco de Coronado explored the American Southwest.

Coronado was born in Spain in 1510. In 1535, Coronado's friend Antonio de
10 Mendoza became viceroy, the leader, of New Spain. New Spain included much of what is today Mexico. Coronado traveled with his friend to New Spain and worked as Mendoza's **assistant**.
15 After his arrival in New Spain, Coronado became an important man. He married Beatriz Estrada, the daughter of a wealthy man. This marriage made Coronado very rich. Coronado's power
20 grew, and he became governor of one of the provinces.

After some time, Mendoza asked Coronado to lead a search for seven **legendary** cities. These cities were called
25 the "Seven Cities of Cibola." People believed that these cities had streets made of gold. Stories also told of tall houses with doors **decorated** with jewels.

In 1540, Coronado took 1,400 men
30 with him to search for these **treasures**. He also took horses for the troops to ride and sheep, cattle, and pigs to feed the men. The explorers searched in what is now the American Southwest. They
35 crossed mountains and found a Native American *pueblo* or village. The Native Americans were the Zuni tribe.

When Coronado found the Zuni pueblo, he found something very
40 unusual. Most of the Zuni homes were built into the cliffs. The Zuni built their homes this way to protect them, but this was not enough to protect the Zuni people from the men on horses and their
45 guns. Coronado **captured** the Zuni pueblo. The **treasure hunters** did not find any gold, so they kept looking. They captured and searched other nearby villages but found nothing.

50 The explorers still did not give up. Coronado sent a small group of men west and another group north. Both groups returned with stories of deep canyons but without gold. Eventually,
55 Coronado realized that the seven cities were probably not real cities, only a legend.

After two years, Coronado and some of his men returned to New Spain.
60 Coronado told Mendoza that he had not found any gold. Mendoza was angry and called Coronado a failure. A court tried Coronado for his failure. They found him innocent of the **charges**. He
65 returned to his role of governor. Later Coronado was tried again. This time the charges were cruelty and dishonesty. The court found him guilty, and Coronado was removed from office. He died that
70 same year in 1544.

Many people thought that Coronado's search for treasure failed, but he and his men found something more important than gold. The men who did not return
75 with Coronado became the first Spanish settlers of the American Southwest. The land he and his men explored is different from other places in the world. The explorers did not find the gold they were
80 looking for. Instead, they found natural treasures like the Grand Canyon and Monument Valley.

Read the passage again and answer the questions. Circle your answers.

MAIN IDEA

1. What is the main topic of the passage?
   A. the search for gold
   B. Coronado's explorations
   C. the life of Antonio Mendoza
   D. Coronado's marriage to Beatriz Estrada

DETAIL

2. Coronado was born
   A. in Mexico
   B. in 1535
   C. in Spain
   D. in 1544

3. The Zuni built special houses
   A. in cliffs
   B. from wood
   C. in Spain
   D. all of the above

4. What did Coronado find on his exploration?
   A. jewels
   B. gold
   C. horses
   D. none of the above

5. Why did Coronado take cattle with him?
   A. as food for his men
   B. to start a ranch
   C. for his men to ride
   D. to carry the supplies

6. Which of the following is **not** true?
   A. Coronado sent some small groups of men to other places to look for treasure.
   B. Coronado found tall houses with doors decorated with jewels.
   C. Coronado found villages built into cliffs.
   D. Coronado was tried more than once.

INFERENCE

7. Which of the following statements is probably true?
   A. Some of Coronado's men stayed in the new land.
   B. Coronado returned with all 1,400 men.
   C. All of Coronado's men were tried with him.
   D. Coronado found gold but didn't tell anyone.

8. What do we know about Coronado?
   A. He was a very good governor.
   B. He was a very honest man.
   C. He wanted to be wealthy.
   D. He was kind to Native Americans.

CHAPTER 2

◀ Monument Valley, Utah

PREPARE TO READ

Discuss these questions.

1. Look at the picture. Describe what you see.

2. Imagine what the first people to see this place thought. Discuss your ideas with a partner.

WORD FOCUS

Match the words with their definitions.

A.
1. amazing ___   **a.** likely to cause injury or damage
2. cactus ___   **b.** the weather conditions of a place
3. canyon ___   **c.** surprising
4. climate ___   **d.** a plant that grows in very dry places
5. dangerous ___   **e.** a deep valley with very steep sides

B.
1. dramatic ___   **a.** something that causes great surprise
2. petroglyph ___   **b.** what is left when a building or town is destroyed or abandoned
3. ruins ___   **c.** an area of land with no signs of human life
4. wilderness ___   **d.** a carving on a rock
5. wonder ___   **e.** exciting or impressive

SCAN

Guess if this is true or false. Circle *a* or *b*.

The Colorado River flows through the Grand Canyon.

a. True   **b.** False

Scan the passage quickly to check your answer.

The American Southwest: Nature's Treasure

The American Southwest does not look like most other places. When Coronado explored this area, he found something much better than gold. He
5 found beautiful sights in nature that no European had ever seen. When people see this area for the first time, they realize how different it is. The red, gold, and brown colors of the earth look
10 **dramatic** against the bright blue sky. The mountains leap out of the desert floor like dancers on a stage.

When people think of the Southwest, they often think of deserts. Some of
15 these deserts are wide and flat, filled with **cactus** and sagebrush. Others have tall dunes of white sand that stretch as far as the eye can see.

One very **dangerous** desert is
20 Death Valley. Temperatures can be as hot as 130°F (54°C). These extreme temperatures make the area impossible to live in. When people visit Death Valley, they can see **ruins** left from people who
25 tried to live in this area. There are old mines and ghost towns in the valley as well as **petroglyphs**, cliff drawings, from the Native Americans who lived there before.

30 The Southwest is not only a flat desert. It is the home of the Grand **Canyon**, which is one of the Natural **Wonders** of the world. It is 277 miles (446 km) long and 15 miles (24 km)
35 wide at its widest point. On average, it is about 4,000 feet (1,200 m) deep, 6,000 (1,800 m) at its deepest. The Colorado River flows through the canyon where it has cut through the stone for millions
40 of years. In the canyon, people can experience several different **climates**. At the bottom of the canyon, there are short desert trees, called "scrub." In the middle of the canyon, there are other
45 desert plants such as cactus and juniper. On the rim, there are pine forests.

Although the Grand Canyon is the largest, there are many canyons in the Southwest. Some of the most beautiful
50 canyons are called "slot" canyons because they are small and narrow. Rivers cutting through the rock form these canyons, which are often only a few feet wide and hundreds of feet deep.

55 Some of the most dramatic sights in the Southwest are the tall stones that reach to the sky in Monument Valley. These tall red rocks stand like statues in the middle of the flat desert.

60 Just as **amazing** is the saguaro cactus. This giant plant is the largest cactus in the world. It can grow to be 50 feet (15 m) tall. It can live for hundreds of years. It grows very slowly. It is often just
65 six inches (15 cm) tall after ten years. The big arms of the plant only begin to grow after 80 years. These heavy plants hold tons of water. These cacti can be seen in Arizona and New Mexico.

70 The beauty of this **wilderness** is unlike any place on Earth. The land in the American Southwest seems as wild today as it was when Spanish explorers traveled across it hundreds of years ago.

Read the passage again and answer the questions. Circle your answers.

MAIN IDEA

1. What is the main topic of the passage?
   A. the amazing Grand Canyon
   B. the beautiful sights of the American Southwest
   C. the explorers of the American Southwest
   D. the life of a saguaro cactus

DETAIL

2. How hot can it get in Death Valley?
   A. 90°F (32°C)
   B. 110°F (43°C)
   C. 130°F (54°C)
   D. 150°F (65.5°C)

3. How long is the Grand Canyon?
   A. 217 miles (349 km)
   B. 237 miles (381 km)
   C. 257 miles (414 km)
   D. 277 miles (446 km)

4. Which of the following is a type of plant?
   A. cactus
   B. juniper
   C. pine
   D. all of the above

5. Which of the following is one of the world's Natural Wonders?
   A. Death Valley
   B. the Grand Canyon
   C. Monument Valley
   D. New Mexico

6. How old is a saguaro cactus before it begins to grow arms?
   A. 6 years
   B. 15 years
   C. 80 years
   D. 100 years

INFERENCE

7. Why did people leave Death Valley?
   A. They didn't like the scenery.
   B. They didn't find any gold.
   C. The climate was too hot.
   D. There were ghosts.

8. Which of the following statements is true about the American Southwest?
   A. It never rains there.
   B. It is always 130°F (54°C) there.
   C. It is all a large flat desert.
   D. It has many different characteristics.

CHAPTER 3

◀ A miner looking for gold

PREPARE TO READ

Discuss these questions.

1. Would you like to go on a hunt for treasure? Why or why not?

2. Where would you go to find treasure? Why?

WORD FOCUS

Match the words with their definitions.

A.

1. ceremony ___   **a.** a fine dry powder made from very small pieces
2. dust ___   **b.** not easily seen or found
3. gem ___   **c.** a place where people remove valuable minerals from the Earth
4. hidden ___   **d.** a formal event to mark something special
5. mine ___   **e.** a jewel or precious stone

B.

1. mineral ___   **a.** a natural substance, especially one that is dug out of the ground
2. perform ___   **b.** a place where water comes up naturally from the ground
3. spring ___   **c.** as people believe or think
4. supposedly ___   **d.** take part in a play, sing, or dance in front of an audience
5. thrive ___   **e.** be very successful

SCAN

Guess if this is true or false. Circle *a* or *b*.

Ponce de Leon explored Alaska.

a. True   **b.** False

Scan the passage quickly to check your answer.

The Search for Treasure

Throughout history, people have always searched for treasure. Legends tell about **hidden** places filled with amazing riches or magic powers.
5 Explorers have spent their entire lives searching for treasure that might or might not really exist.

Early stories told of seven cities filled with gold, silver, and jewels. The streets
10 were **supposedly** paved with gold. Two men who searched for these cities were Fernando de Vaca and Francisco de Coronado. Both searched for the seven cities in the 1500s. De Vaca explored
15 the area around the states of Texas and Kansas. De Vaca never found the cities, and Coronado searched again a few years later in the American Southwest. Coronado found several Native
20 American villages but no gold. No one has ever found even one of these seven legendary cities.

Other explorers have searched for the famed city of El Dorado, "The Golden
25 One." Treasure hunters thought this was a city in South America. One legend is that El Dorado was not a city, but the name of a king who covered his body in gold **dust**. The king's people threw
30 gold and **gems** such as emeralds into the water as the king floated by on a raft. It is said that native South Americans **performed** a **ceremony** like this in Colombia. A tiny gold raft with a man
35 standing on it was found there. The raft is on display in the Gold Museum in Bogotá. Despite such interesting clues, no one has ever found El Dorado.

Another search was for the Fountain
40 of Youth. Stories tell about a magic **spring** that makes old people young again. Spanish settlers in the Caribbean heard these stories. In 1513, Ponce de Leon searched unsuccessfully for this
45 spring in what is now Florida.

In the 1800s, the search for gold continued in the western United States. Thousands of people rushed to the American West, especially to California
50 and Alaska. This search was called the "Gold Rush." People hoped to find their fortune in gold. Some people did find gold and silver, but most did not. Cities like San Francisco and Anchorage grew
55 as a result of the arrival of so many people.

During this same period, many valuable **minerals** were found in the American Southwest. Large silver,
60 copper, and gold **mines thrived** for a time. This was the same area where Coronado searched unsuccessfully. The explorers' plan was to take the treasures from those who had it. Much of the land
65 did hold great mineral treasures, but they were found long after the explorers were gone.

People today still search for treasure. Some people search for ships that sank
70 in the ocean. Others look for lost mines or treasures buried by pirates. Some people even search in unusual places such as garage sales and flea markets. They hope to find some rare treasure
75 hidden in the junk. Many people believe the old saying, "One man's trash is another man's treasure."

Read the passage again and answer the questions. Circle your answers.

MAIN IDEA

1. What is the main topic of the passage?
   A. the search for the seven cities of gold
   B. the search for treasure
   C. the search for the Fountain of Youth
   D. why no one ever found gold

DETAIL

2. What did Coronado find in his search for treasure?
   A. several Native American villages
   B. the seven cities of gold
   C. the Fountain of Youth
   D. gold

3. What was El Dorado?
   A. a legendary city in South America
   B. a king who covered his body in gold
   C. a legendary treasure that was never found
   D. all of the above

4. What city grew because of the Gold Rush?
   A. Boston
   B. San Francisco
   C. Miami
   D. New York

5. Who searched for the Fountain of Youth?
   A. Fernando de Vaca
   B. Ponce de Leon
   C. Francisco de Coronado
   D. El Dorado

6. How many of the seven cities of gold have explorers found?
   A. zero
   B. two
   C. four
   D. all seven

INFERENCE

7. Which of the following statements is true?
   A. El Dorado might be a person or a place.
   B. The Spanish explorers found El Dorado.
   C. People believed that the Fountain of Youth makes young people old.
   D. The Spanish explorers were only a legend.

8. "One man's trash is another man's treasure" means
   A. You can always find something valuable at a garage sale.
   B. People dig through trash to find gold.
   C. Things that some people think are worthless are valuable to others.
   D. all of the above

VOCABULARY REVIEW

WHICH MEANING?

From Chapter 1: *Francisco de Coronado: Explorer*

1. What does the word *try* mean in this context?

> A court tried Coronado for his failure.

A. try *(verb)* make an effort to do something
B. try *(verb)* decide if someone is guilty of a crime
C. try *(verb)* test something to see how well it works

From Chapter 2: *The American Southwest: Nature's Treasure*

2. What does the word *extreme* mean in this context?

> These extreme temperatures make the area impossible to live in.

A. extreme *(adjective)* not the usual or moderate political view
B. extreme *(noun)* something that is completely different from or opposite something else
C. extreme *(adjective)* the greatest or strongest possible

From Chapter 3: *The Search for Treasure*

3. What does the word *fortune* mean in this context?

> People hoped to find their fortune in gold.

A. fortune *(noun)* a very large amount of money
B. fortune *(noun)* something that will happen to someone in the future
C. fortune *(noun)* the power that affects what happens in a person's life

WRONG WORD

One word in each group does not fit. Circle the word.

1. dramatic	amazing	climate	beautiful
2. fortune	treasure	gem	ceremony
3. mine	extreme	mineral	gold
4. wilderness	governor	assistant	explorer
5. legendary	plant	cactus	tree
6. canyon	wilderness	desert	miner

Fill in the blanks with words from each box.

ceremony	decorated	hidden	legendary	spring

1. The water from the _____ was cool and delicious.
2. They searched unsuccessfully for the _____ treasure.
3. The wedding _____ took place in the garden.
4. The door of the house was _____ with gold and silver. It was beautiful.
5. The woman was famous for her face. Her beauty was _____.

assistant	captured	extreme	minerals	wilderness

6. The old miner searched for _____ such as copper and silver.
7. I hired an _____ because I needed someone to help me.
8. The park rangers _____ the bear that had chased the hikers.
9. The _____ heat of Death Valley made it impossible to live there.
10. Many people enjoy hiking and camping in the _____.

climate	dangerous	gem	tried	thrived

11. The diamond is the most common _____ in wedding rings.
12. The _____ of the American Southwest is hot and dry.
13. The thief was _____ in court. He was found guilty of theft.
14. Rock climbing can be a _____ sport. It's important to be careful.
15. The plants _____ in the warm climate.

WORD FAMILIES

Fill in the blanks with words from each box.

explore *(verb)*	exploration *(noun)*	explorer *(noun)*

1. The scouts will _____ the mountains with their guide.
2. Coronado was a famous _____ who searched the American Southwest for gold.

| danger *(noun)* | dangerous *(adjective)* | dangerously *(adverb)* |

3. The hikers got _____ close to the edge of the canyon.

4. They were in _____, so they called for help.

| assist *(verb)* | assistance *(noun)* | assistant *(noun)* |

5. A student loan gives financial _____ to someone who wants to go to college.

6. A dictionary can _____ you in finding the meaning of words.

WRAP IT UP

DISCUSS THE THEME

Read these questions and discuss them with a partner.

1. Do you like to explore new places? Where have you gone? What unusual places or things did you find?

2. Do you know of any modern-day explorers? Where do they go? What do they look for?

3. What do you consider an adventure? Have you ever had an adventure?

4. What stories have you heard about people searching for treasure? Were the treasure hunters successful?

RESPOND IN WRITING

Look back at the unit and choose the passage you enjoyed the most. Read it again. Write a short summary of the passage.

_____

_____

_____

_____

_____

What do you think is the most interesting thing about this passage, and why?
Write a short paragraph.

_____

_____

_____

_____

_____

_____

UNIT 6

U.S. HISTORY
CRIME AND PUNISHMENT

▲ A scene from the 1920s

BEFORE YOU READ

Answer these questions.

1. Look at the photo. Describe what you see.

2. What do you think these men did for a living?

3. What do you think the phrase "organized crime" means?

71

CHAPTER 1

◀ Al Capone, 1899–1947

PREPARE TO READ

Discuss these questions.

1. Look at the picture of Al Capone. What do you know about him?

2. What do you think he was like? Why do you think he was famous?

WORD FOCUS

Match the words with their definitions.

A.

1. arrest _____   **a.** a person who is in jail or prison

2. crime _____   **b.** a violent criminal in a gang

3. gangster _____   **c.** against the law

4. illegal _____   **d.** an illegal act

5. inmate _____   **e.** take someone prisoner

B.

1. peak _____   **a.** rich

2. put away _____   **b.** opponent

3. release _____   **c.** the highest point or amount

4. rival _____   **d.** let someone or something go

5. wealthy _____   **e.** put someone in prison *(slang)*

SCAN

Guess if this is true or false. Circle *a* or *b*.

Al Capone was born in Chicago.

a. True   **b.** False

Scan the passage quickly to check your answer.

Al Capone: A Life of Crime

When people hear the name Al Capone, they think: **gangster**, Chicago, organized **crime**. Capone was famous for his life of crime, which started at a young age in New York. He reached the **peak** of his power in Chicago in the 1920s.

Capone was born January 17, 1899 in Brooklyn, New York. At age 14, he quit school. He joined a gang with his school friend, Charles "Lucky" Luciano. One night, Capone said something about a guy's sister, and the guy cut Capone's face with a knife. After that, he was called "Scar Face."

In 1920, Capone traveled to Chicago. This was the time of Prohibition in the United States. A law had made all alcoholic drinks **illegal**. Bootleggers made and sold beer and whiskey illegally. Capone's power grew, and by 1924 he controlled both bootlegging and gambling in Chicago. His illegal activities brought in over $100,000 a week. In the 1920s, that made him a very rich man.

Capone became known as a leader in Chicago. He was **wealthy** and powerful. He did a few good things. He helped poor people and gave money to schools, but people still feared him. Even government officials were afraid of him. He could do whatever he wanted, good or bad.

The situation changed after an event called the St. Valentine's Day Massacre in February 1929. By 1929, Capone had over $62,000,000 hidden away. His main **rival** was George "Bugs" Morane, another bootlegger. Capone ordered one of his men to kill him. "Bugs" escaped, but seven of his men were killed. The story of the massacre spread across the country. Capone had gone too far; he had to be stopped.

The federal government decided to go after Capone. They tried several times to **put** him **away**. Each time he was set free after only a short time. Then, in 1931, the government **arrested** him for not paying taxes and for bootlegging. They sent him to prison for eleven years. He also had to pay a fine of $50,000 and all the taxes he owed.

The government sent Capone to a prison in Atlanta, Georgia. Even in prison he was powerful. He kept a lot of money with him. He paid the guards to take care of him. They brought him anything he wanted. He even had nice furniture.

In 1934, the government sent Capone to Alcatraz, a prison in California. This prison was for serious criminals. The government took away the things he had enjoyed in prison in Atlanta. Capone tried to build his power at Alcatraz. He tried to give the guards money, but it didn't work. The government had finally managed to control Capone.

Capone spent four and a half years as one of Alcatraz's most famous **inmates**. He lived a quiet life in prison. He was **released** from prison in 1939. His health was poor, so he didn't go back to Chicago. Instead, he moved to Florida, where he lived quietly with his family until his death in 1947. His life of crime was over at the age of just 48.

Read the passage again and answer the questions. Circle your answers.

MAIN IDEA

1. What is the main topic of this passage?
   A. organized crime in the U.S.
   B. the Prohibition Era
   C. New York gangs
   D. Al Capone's life

DETAIL

2. How did Al Capone become rich?
   A. He did many good things.
   B. He controlled bootlegging in Chicago.
   C. Gambling was illegal.
   D. He helped poor people.

3. When was the St. Valentine's Day Massacre?
   A. 1920
   B. 1929
   C. 1934
   D. 1957

4. What happened in 1931?
   A. Al Capone was sent to Alcatraz.
   B. The government moved him from Atlanta.
   C. Al Capone was sent to prison for eleven years.
   D. Al Capone wanted to live like other prisoners.

5. How much did Al Capone make in a week in the 1920s?
   A. $100
   B. $1,000
   C. $10,000
   D. none of the above

6. Al Capone was sent to prison for 11 years for
   A. not paying taxes
   B. killing people
   C. robbing banks
   D. giving money to prison guards

INFERENCE

7. Why was the St. Valentine's Day Massacre important?
   A. It was in February.
   B. "Bugs" Morane was a rival.
   C. It made the government decide to stop Al Capone.
   D. Al Capone had over $62,000,000.

8. The most important thing about Al Capone's move to Alcatraz was
   A. his health was poor
   B. his crime career was over
   C. he went to Florida after that
   D. he died in Florida with his family

CHAPTER 2

◀ Alcatraz prison, California

PREPARE TO READ

Discuss these questions.

1. Look at the picture of Alcatraz. What do you know about this prison?

2. Why do you think Alcatraz is famous?

WORD FOCUS

Match the words with their definitions.

A.
1. austere ___   **a.** brag; talk to make people admire you
2. boast ___   **b.** very plain and simple
3. cell ___   **c.** difficult to follow or deal with
4. complicated ___ **d.** the small room where a prisoner is kept
5. drown ___   **e.** die under water

B.
1. ideal ___   **a.** be all around something or someone
2. infamous ___   **b.** best possible
3. prison ___   **c.** well known for being bad
4. surround ___   **d.** a building where criminals are kept
5. transfer ___   **e.** move someone or something to another place

SCAN

Guess if this is true or false. Circle *a* or *b*.

A lot of prisoners escaped from Alcatraz.

a. True   **b.** False

Scan the passage quickly to check your answer.

Alcatraz

Alcatraz sits on an island in San Francisco Bay off the California coast. This **infamous prison** operated from the 1930s until the middle of the
5 1960s. Alcatraz prison was known as "The Rock." The worst criminals in the United States were sent there. Today, Alcatraz is a national park, and people visit the island on tours to see what life
10 was like for the inmates.

The island was named by a Spanish explorer in 1775. He called the island "Isla de Alcatraces," which means "Pelican Island." The island was an **ideal**
15 place for a prison. It was **surrounded** by very cold water, and it was far away from land. It was impossible to escape from Alcatraz by swimming. The water was too cold to survive in for long, and
20 it was over a mile to the shore.

The prison was cold and **austere**. The prisoners lived in very small **cells**. Each cell had one bed, a sink with only cold water, and a toilet. The prisoners
25 could not talk to each other except at meals or during a short recreation time outside. Otherwise, there was a rule of silence. About 300 men were imprisoned on Alcatraz at one time. Inmates stayed
30 about eight years.

With nothing to do, most prisoners thought about ways to escape. The government claims no inmate was ever successful, but they cannot be sure.
35 The most famous escape attempt was in 1962. Three men got away. They were Frank Morris and two brothers, John and Clarence Anglin. They disappeared from their cells and were never seen
40 again. The guards said they **drowned**, but no one knows for sure. Prison officials do know the men had a very **complicated** escape plan. The men even took raincoats to use as life vests
45 in the water. Several days after they disappeared, a body was found in the water. However, the guards couldn't identify the person. A packet with photographs of the Anglin family was
50 also found. No one knows if the men drowned or escaped in a boat.

There were many famous inmates at Alcatraz. Probably the most famous is Robert Stroud. He was called the Bird
55 Man of Alcatraz because he raised and studied birds in his prison cell. He was imprisoned at Alcatraz from 1942 to 1959. He became an expert on birds. Another famous inmate was George
60 "Machine Gun" Kelly. He was one of the most well-known gangsters from the Prohibition Era. He, like Al Capone, was a bootlegger. He was sent to prison in Kansas, but he kept **boasting** that
65 he would escape. The government **transferred** him to Alcatraz. There he became a model prisoner, like Al Capone.

No prisoner wanted to serve his time
70 on Alcatraz. For almost 40 years, it was the final stop for the worst criminals. The prison was eventually closed because it was too old and too difficult to maintain. Today tourists come to
75 imagine the lives of the inmates who once were imprisoned on this rocky island.

Read the passage again and answer the questions. Circle your answers.

MAIN IDEA

1. What is the main topic of this passage?
   A. how to escape from prison
   B. why Al Capone was sent to Alcatraz
   C. famous inmates in history
   D. the history of Alcatraz

DETAIL

2. The island was ideal for a prison because
   A. its name comes from Spanish
   B. its name means "Pelican Island"
   C. it is surrounded by water
   D. it was discovered in 1775

3. The rule of silence meant
   A. the cells were very small
   B. there were 300 men there
   C. prisoners could not talk to each other
   D. inmates could touch both walls

4. Which of the following is another name for Alcatraz?
   A. Bird Island
   B. Machine Gun
   C. The Rock
   D. Anglin Island

5. The Bird Man of Alcatraz was famous because
   A. he was Robert Stroud
   B. he raised and studied birds in prison
   C. he was in prison from 1942 to 1959
   D. he was there with Al Capone

6. Alcatraz was closed because
   A. of its age
   B. it was inexpensive to maintain
   C. the prisoners didn't like it
   D. all of the above

INFERENCE

7. What is true about Frank Morris?
   A. He probably drowned.
   B. His body was found in the water.
   C. He was alone.
   D. His brothers escaped with him.

8. Prisoners did **not** want to go to Alcatraz because
   A. life was difficult there
   B. they were only allowed to talk at special times
   C. the cells were so small and cold
   D. all of the above

CHAPTER 3

J. Edgar Hoover, Director of the FBI from 1924–1972

PREPARE TO READ

Discuss these questions.

1. Have you heard of the FBI? What do the letters stand for?
2. What kind of work does the FBI do?

WORD FOCUS

Match the words with their definitions.

A.

1. associate ___   **a.** written or spoken words against someone
2. criticism ___   **b.** have
3. cross ___   **c.** go from one side to the other
4. federal ___   **d.** find a connection between two things
5. hold ___   **e.** relating to the central government

B.

1. improve ___   **a.** agreement with someone's actions
2. investigate ___   **b.** find someone or something after looking for a long time
3. support ___   **c.** believe in someone or something
4. track down ___   **d.** make something better
5. trust ___   **e.** try to find out the truth

SCAN

Guess if this is true or false. Circle *a* or *b*.

The FBI is almost 100 years old.

a. True   **b.** False

Scan the passage quickly to check your answer.

The FBI

The FBI (**Federal** Bureau of Investigation) is the agency that fights serious crimes in the United States. It **investigates** organized crime, drug trafficking, bank robbery, certain murders, and kidnapping. It also investigates computer crimes and white-collar crimes, non-violent crimes against businesses.

The agency that became the FBI began on July 26, 1908. It was part of the U.S. Department of Justice. The agency started out with only 34 agents. Today there are thousands of agents. It got its current name, the FBI, in 1935.

In its early years, the FBI mainly helped city and state police fight crime. But, as organized crime grew, so did the FBI. Organized crime is when a group of criminals work together to do illegal things.

Gangsters like Al Capone were members of well-organized gangs of criminals. Early in the last century, organized crime had spread across the United States. The government had a difficult time fighting it. This was because most laws were state laws, not federal laws. The police could not **cross** state lines to investigate a crime. A criminal would just leave the state, and the police couldn't do anything.

Organized crime was very active in the 1920s during Prohibition. In 1920, the government passed a law to make it illegal to buy or sell alcohol. But people still wanted alcohol, and organized crime quickly became involved. Illegal alcohol was one reason Al Capone and other gangsters were so successful. In 1933, the government ended Prohibition. After that, organized crime gangs found other ways to make money.

J. Edgar Hoover became director of the FBI in 1924. Many people **associate** his name with the FBI. As the director, he worked hard to **improve** the agency. He wanted to make it easier for the FBI to catch criminals. He hired new agents and made sure they were well trained. He got new laws passed. Hoover did not like **criticism**, and he fired people who disagreed with him. But Hoover had a lot of public **support**. The FBI became known for its honest, hard-working agents. The public **trusted** the FBI. Hoover's agents were called "G-men" during this time. "G-men" stood for "government men."

In 1934, Congress made bank robbery and other serious crimes federal crimes. This meant the FBI could now cross state lines to investigate crimes and catch criminals. This gave the "G-men" more powers to **track down** criminals. In 1934, the new laws allowed the FBI to capture three well-known gangsters: John Dillinger, Charles "Pretty Boy" Floyd, and "Baby Face" Nelson.

Hoover was the director of the FBI for 48 years. Some people felt that he had too much power for too long a time. After he died, a law was passed that the director could only **hold** the job for 10 years. Over time, federal laws have given the FBI more power to fight crime and catch criminals. Today, the FBI is able to investigate crime at all levels and across all state lines.

Read the passage again and answer the questions. Circle your answers.

MAIN IDEA

1. What is the main topic of this passage?
   A. types of organized crime
   B. how the FBI developed
   C. organized crime during Prohibition
   D. how Dillinger was caught

DETAIL

2. What does FBI stand for?
   A. Federation Bureau of Investigators
   B. Federated Business Investigators
   C. Federal Business Incorporated
   D. Federal Bureau of Investigation

3. When did the FBI get its name?
   A. 1908
   B. 1919
   C. 1920
   D. 1935

4. What was it illegal to do after 1920?
   A. cross state lines
   B. investigate a crime
   C. buy or sell alcohol
   D. all of the above

5. The most important change in 1934 was
   A. Hoover's men were called G-men
   B. organized crime had new ways to make money
   C. Congress made serious crimes federal crimes
   D. agents captured "Baby Face" Nelson

6. Which of the following is **not** true?
   A. The public supported Hoover.
   B. FBI agents were trusted.
   C. Some people felt Hoover was too powerful.
   D. Hoover took criticism well.

INFERENCE

7. Why was it easier for the FBI to catch criminals after 1934?
   A. Organized crime had spread.
   B. There were G-men.
   C. Federal laws had changed.
   D. "Machine Gun" Kelley was caught.

8. The most important thing about Hoover's career was
   A. he hired many people
   B. he improved the FBI in many ways
   C. he was the director for 48 years
   D. he became the director in 1924

VOCABULARY REVIEW

WHICH MEANING?

From Chapter 1: *Al Capone: A Life of Crime*

1. What does *free* mean in this context?

> Each time he was set free after only a short time.

A. free *(adjective)* no longer a prisoner
B. free *(adjective)* costing nothing
C. free *(adjective)* without appointments

From Chapter 2: *Alcatraz*

2. What does *model* mean in this context?

> There he became a model prisoner, like Al Capone.

A. model *(noun)* a small copy of something
B. model *(noun)* a person employed to wear clothes
C. model *(noun)* a perfect example

From Chapter 3: *The FBI*

3. What does *power* mean in this context?

> This gave the FBI more powers to track down people.

A. power *(noun)* energy
B. power *(noun)* natural ability
C. power *(noun)* authority

WRONG WORD

One word in each group does not fit. Circle the word.

1. gangster	inmate	criminal	police
2. bootlegging	gambling	put away	kidnapping
3. wealthy	powerful	poor	rich
4. survive	prisoner	inmate	guard
5. claim	drown	boast	say
6. famous	well-known	successful	trust

WORDS IN CONTEXT

Fill in the blanks with words from each box.

gangster	illegal	released	rivals	wealthy

1. Al Capone was a well-known _____ during Prohibition.
2. Buying and selling alcohol was _____ during Prohibition.
3. Al Capone became very _____ during his life of crime.
4. Gangsters like Al Capone often had their _____ killed.
5. Al Capone was _____ from prison in 1939. Then he joined his family.

boasted	complicated	ideal	surrounded	transferred

6. The police _____ the bank robbers and captured them.
7. The island was _____ for a prison because of the cold water around it.
8. Three prisoners had a very _____ escape plan and were never seen again.
9. The guards _____ the inmate from another prison to Alcatraz.
10. In Kansas, Kelly _____ he would escape. He told everyone he would.

criticism	federal	hold	investigated	tracked down

11. The FBI _____ the crime. They wanted to find out who did it.
12. Hoover felt that state laws were too weak. He wanted _____ laws instead.
13. Now the director of the FBI cannot _____ the position for as long as Hoover did.
14. Hoover didn't like to hear any _____ about how he ran the FBI.
15. More criminals were _____ after 1934. The laws made it easier to catch them.

WORD FAMILIES

Fill in the blanks with words from each box.

crime (*noun*)	criminal (*noun*)	criminally (*adverb*)

1. Robbing a bank is a serious _____.
2. The _____ was sent to prison for many years.

prisoner *(noun)*	prison *(noun)*	imprison *(verb)*

3. Many inmates wanted to escape from the _____.

4. The government decided to _____ Capone on Alcatraz.

support *(verb)*	supporter *(noun)*	support *(noun)*

5. The FBI had a lot of public _____ during Hoover's time. People trusted the agency.

6. Hoover was a strong _____ of federal laws for serious crimes.

WRAP IT UP

DISCUSS THE THEME

Read these questions and discuss them with your partner.

1. Which crimes do you think are the most serious?

2. What types of punishment do you think work? Does your partner agree with you?

3. What do you think the expression "crime doesn't pay" means? Do you think this was true for Al Capone? Give reasons.

4. What should a prison be like? What should inmates be allowed to do?

RESPOND IN WRITING

Look back at the unit and choose the passage you enjoyed the most. Read it again. Write a short summary of the passage.

_____

_____

_____

_____

_____

What do you think is the most interesting thing about this passage, and why? Write a short paragraph.

_____

_____

_____

_____

_____

_____

_____

LATIN AMERICAN STUDIES
NATIONAL TREASURES

BEFORE YOU READ

Answer these questions.

1. What does the term "Latin America" mean?

2. What are some famous places in Latin America? Why are they famous?

3. If you had the chance to visit Latin America, where would you like to go? Why?

CHAPTER 1

◀ Gabriela Sabatini, 1970–

PREPARE TO READ

Discuss these questions.

1. Can you name any famous tennis players?
2. What do professional athletes do after they retire from sports?

WORD FOCUS

Match the words with their definitions.

A.

1. afford ___
2. bring out ___
3. career ___
4. consider ___
5. decline ___

a. become weaker, smaller, or less good
b. have enough money for something
c. a job or profession for which you trained
d. think about something in a particular way
e. produce or cause something to appear

B.

1. glamorous ___
2. in honor of ___
3. line ___
4. proud ___
5. top ___

a. pleased and satisfied
b. attractive and full of excitement
c. out of respect for
d. a type of product
e. the highest in position

SCAN

Guess if this is true or false. Circle *a* or *b*.

Gabriela Sabatini was always a businesswoman.

a. True   b. False

Scan the passage quickly to check your answer.

Gabriela Sabatini: Life after Tennis

The life of a professional athlete seems **glamorous**. Professional athletes are often famous, and they make a lot of money. But an athlete's life is also
5 extremely difficult. Few people are good enough to be a professional athlete. Gabriela Sabatini of Argentina was one of those few people. She became a professional tennis player when she was
10 just 14 years old.

Most athletes play a sport as long as they can. Athletic **careers** are usually short, so athletes work as long as possible. Some athletes keep playing
15 because they don't know what to do next. Gabriela Sabatini was a little different. She had a plan.

Sabatini grew up in Argentina. She started playing tennis when she was
20 about six years old. Other children didn't want to play tennis with her because she was a much better player. So she hit the ball against a wall and waited for her chance. Later, she found
25 good tennis partners and coaches. In just a few years, she became one of the world's best tennis players.

Sabatini played professional tennis for 12 years and earned nearly nine million
30 dollars. She was one of the **top** three women's tennis players in the world. Sabatini was only 20 years old when she won the U.S. Open championship in 1990. She was popular among the other
35 players. Monica Seles, another tennis champion, said Sabatini always **brought out** the best in other people.

Gabriela Sabatini enjoyed her career, but over time she lost her love of the
40 sport. She also had some injuries.

After the U.S. Open championship, her abilities **declined**. She didn't win many tournaments. Sometimes, she could not play because she was hurt. Soon, many
45 other women were better at tennis.

In 1996, at age 26, Gabriela Sabatini retired from professional tennis. Her fans, other tennis players, and people in Argentina were sad. The front pages of
50 newspapers in Argentina carried many stories about Sabatini and her career. People in Argentina **considered** her a national treasure.

Sabatini was not unhappy about
55 retiring from tennis. This was part of her plan. She wanted to do other things with her life. At 26, Sabatini was a very beautiful and glamorous woman. She had long, thick, black hair. She was
60 tall and in good shape physically. She became a model late in her tennis career. Companies hired her to be in ads for their products.

She enjoyed the world of fashion and
65 cosmetics. She worked with a company to make her own **line** of perfumes. Her first perfume was called "Gabriela Sabatini." It was so popular that she developed others. She even created one
70 perfume **in honor of** Argentina. It is called "Temperamento."

Sabatini is very **proud** of her country. She loves Argentinean music and the tango, one of Argentina's favorite dances.
75 She has traveled all over the world as a tennis player and as a businesswoman. She can **afford** to live anywhere. But she chooses to spend most of her time in Buenos Aires, her hometown.

Read the passage again and answer the questions. Circle your answers.

MAIN IDEA

1. What is the main topic of the passage?
   A. a famous tennis player who is still winning championships
   B. a famous tennis player who is now a successful businesswoman
   C. a famous tennis player who retired and didn't do anything else
   D. a famous model who is now a professional tennis player

DETAIL

2. Other children didn't want to play tennis with Sabatini because
   A. she was too good
   B. she had a bad temper
   C. she wasn't friendly
   D. all of the above

3. When did Sabatini become a professional tennis player?
   A. when she was about 6 years old
   B. when she was just 14 years old
   C. when she was only 20 years old
   D. at age 26

4. What did Monica Seles say about Sabatini?
   A. Sabatini brought out the best in other players.
   B. Sabatini was a beautiful model in ads for products.
   C. Sabatini made wonderful perfumes.
   D. Sabatini was an unpopular tennis player.

5. Sabatini created "Temperamento" in honor of
   A. her best friend
   B. her mother
   C. her country
   D. the tango

6. Which of the following statements is true?
   A. The people of Argentina were sad when Sabatini retired.
   B. Sabatini retired from tennis at age 29.
   C. Sabatini made a lot of money doing the tango.
   D. Her perfumes have not been very popular.

INFERENCE

7. Sabatini had a plan because
   A. the career of professional athletes is usually short
   B. no one wanted to play against her
   C. she found good tennis partners and coaches
   D. she won the U.S. Open tennis championship

8. Sabatini lives in Buenos Aires, Argentina, because
   A. she can afford to live anywhere in the world
   B. she enjoyed the world of fashion and cosmetics
   C. she is proud of her country and wants to live there
   D. she wanted to retire from tennis

CHAPTER 2

◀ Machu Picchu, Peru

PREPARE TO READ

Discuss these questions.

1. Do you know about any "lost" cities? When were they "found"?
2. What are some possible reasons that people leave a city and forget it?

WORD FOCUS

Match the words with their definitions.

A.

1. ancient ___
2. column ___
3. fragile ___
4. fuel ___
5. guide ___

a. someone or something that shows you the way
b. easy to damage or break
c. material that produces energy
d. a tall vertical stone structure
e. connected with the distant past; very old

B.

1. lost ___
2. mystery ___
3. raise ___
4. survivor ___
5. wear down ___

a. something that is difficult to understand or explain
b. impossible to find
c. become smaller after use or time
d. make a plant or animal grow so that you can use it
e. someone who does not die in a dangerous situation

SCAN

Guess if this is true or false. Circle *a* or *b*.

Machu Picchu is in a busy city area.

a. True   **b.** False

Scan the passage quickly to check your answer.

Machu Picchu

The **ancient** village of Machu Picchu is one of the most popular tourist destinations in South America. It is in Peru, high in the Andes Mountains, 8,000 feet (2,400 m) above sea level. At one time, about 1,200 people lived in Machu Picchu. After the people left, the village was **lost** and forgotten for hundreds of years. Hiram Bingham, an explorer from the United States, found the ruins in 1911.

The Inca people built Machu Picchu about 500 years ago. The Incas knew how to make good use of the land. Machu Picchu fits the shape of the mountain. The Incas built the village this way to protect it from harsh weather.

The village contains 200 buildings. Houses are in groups, and each house has a large courtyard inside its walls. The Incas used the areas outside the groups of houses to grow corn and potatoes and to **raise** animals. The Incas were very good at building strong walls. Visitors to Machu Picchu still cannot fit a knife between the stones of a village home.

In the center of the village, the Incas built a tall stone **column**, called *intihuatana*. They held a special ceremony there every year before winter came. When winter comes, days become shorter. In their ceremony, the Incas tied the sun to the column. They wanted to hold the sun and keep the long days of summer.

Machu Picchu seemed to be a healthy, busy village. So why was it lost? That is a **mystery**, but experts have some ideas. Machu Picchu was hard to reach. Few people outside the village knew about it. Experts think that many residents died of disease. Others fought a war. The **survivors** left the village. When Spanish soldiers came to South America and attacked other Inca villages, Machu Picchu was already empty.

After Bingham found Machu Picchu in 1911, news of the beautiful village in the Andes traveled quickly around the world. Tourists soon followed. Machu Picchu was still difficult to reach. At first, tourists needed local **guides** to lead them on a four-day hike up a 27-mile (43 km) trail. Today, they can take a train or a bus. Tourists spend 40 million U.S. dollars every year in Peru to visit the famous ruins.

The tourists are good for Peru's economy, but they are not good for Machu Picchu. The village is old and **fragile**. Tourists damage the ruins. Thousands of footsteps from visitors **wear down** the walkways in the village. Salt and oil from people's hands damage the walls. Air pollution from buses hurts the stones. Tourists do not want to damage the village, but they want to see this beautiful, ancient place.

The Peruvian government and conservation groups are trying to solve the problem. A group from the United Nations wants to limit the number of tourists each year. They also want cars and buses to use cleaner **fuel**.

Machu Picchu is a wonderful place to study an ancient culture, but people must respect the land and village, like the Incas did. Everyone must help preserve Machu Picchu so that many more generations can visit Peru's "lost" village.

Read the passage again and answer the questions. Circle your answers.

MAIN IDEA

1. What is the main topic of the passage?
   A. an ancient city in Peru
   B. a new city in Peru
   C. tourists in Peru
   D. the people of Peru

DETAIL

2. Which of the following statements is true?
   A. Machu Picchu has courtyards with walls.
   B. Machu Picchu is about 1,200 years old.
   C. Machu Picchu is high in the mountains of Ecuador.
   D. Machu Picchu is found at 800 feet (240 m) above sea level.

3. What crops did the Incas grow?
   A. rice and beans
   B. tomatoes and peppers
   C. wheat and peas
   D. potatoes and corn

4. How much in dollars do tourists spend to visit Machu Picchu each year?
   A. 27 million
   B. 40 million
   C. 200 million
   D. 800 million

5. What probably happened to the people of Machu Picchu?
   A. They died of disease.
   B. They died in war.
   C. They moved to other places.
   D. all of the above

6. Which of the following does **not** damage the ruins?
   A. air pollution
   B. feet on the walkways
   C. the shape of the land
   D. hands on the walls

INFERENCE

7. How do we know that Incas were good at building walls?
   A. The Incas knew how to make good use of the land.
   B. Visitors still cannot fit a knife between the stones.
   C. Footsteps wear down the walkways in the village.
   D. Hiram Bingham discovered the ruins in 1911.

8. Why does Machu Picchu need help from conservation groups?
   A. Tourists are damaging the ruins.
   B. Tourists want buses to use cleaner fuel.
   C. Tourists must hike for four days to reach the ruins.
   D. Tourists are good for Peru's economy.

CHAPTER 3

The Panama Canal

PREPARE TO READ

Discuss these questions.

1. What do you know about the Panama Canal?
2. Why did people want to build this canal in Panama?

WORD FOCUS

Match the words with their definitions.

A.
1. engineer ___
2. explosive ___
3. feed ___
4. gravity ___
5. journey ___

a. the natural force that makes things move downward
b. a trip
c. a person who designs practical things such as machines and roads
d. put something into something else
e. a substance that can explode like a bomb

B.
1. man-made ___
2. series ___
3. shortcut ___
4. toll ___
5. vary ___

a. a more direct way to go somewhere or do something
b. money that you pay to use a road or bridge
c. made by people, not by nature
d. a number of things that come after each other
e. change at different times

SCAN

Guess if this is true or false. Circle *a* or *b*.

The Panama Canal is at the bottom of South America.

a. True   **b.** False

Scan the passage quickly to check your answer.

The Panama Canal

The Panama Canal is almost 100 years old, but it is still a wonder of technology. The canal is a 50-mile-long (80 km) waterway through the Central American country of Panama. It is a **shortcut** between the Atlantic and Pacific oceans.

Before the canal opened in 1914, ships going from one coast of North or South America to the other had to sail all the way around the bottom of South America. By using the Panama Canal, a ship going from Boston to San Francisco, or the other way, cuts about 8,000 miles (12,800 km) from the **journey**. This saves companies time and money. Then they can sell their goods at a lower cost.

On a map, Panama looks like a thin strip of land connecting Central and South America. It is thin, but it is not flat. **Engineers** had to think of a way to lift ships over the mountainous land. Their solution was to build a **series** of locks. A lock is a huge chamber of water. Each chamber is 1,000 feet long (305 m), 110 feet wide (34 m), and about 85 feet deep (26 m). The locks work together like an elevator.

Building the canal was dangerous and hard work. It took many years. Workers had to use dangerous **explosives** to break through rock. Insects carried diseases that made the workers ill. But when the workers finished the job, they were very proud of the result.

Engineers designed the canal so that **gravity** moves water from one lock to another. A ship moves into the first lock at sea level. A wall closes behind the ship. Canal workers then let water flow into the first lock from the second lock. This water lifts the ship up one level. Workers open the wall in front of the ship, and it moves into the second lock. Then workers use water from the third lock to lift the ship again.

They repeat the process until the ship is level with Gatún Lake in the middle of Panama. Gatún Lake was the largest **man-made** body of water in the world when the Panama Canal opened. Water from a river **feeds** the lake and all the locks. On the other side of the lake, more locks move the ship down to sea level again.

A trip from the entrance of the canal to the exit takes eight to ten hours. A speedboat once made it through the Panama Canal in less than three hours. Ships pay **tolls** to use the Panama Canal. The toll **varies**, depending on the size and shape of the ship. In 1928, a man swam across the Panama Canal. He paid a toll of 36 cents.

The Panama Canal is open every day. About 14,000 ships use the canal every year. It is a safe way to move the big ships. There are few accidents. The United States operated the Panama Canal Zone until 1977. The Republic of Panama took full control of the Panama Canal in 1999. It was a big moment in Panama's history. The canal that carried its name finally belonged to Panama.

Read the passage again and answer the questions. Circle your answers.

MAIN IDEA

1. What is the main topic of the passage?
   A. shipping products from Boston to San Francisco
   B. the Central American country of Panama
   C. the largest man-made body of water in the world
   D. a shortcut between the Atlantic and Pacific oceans

DETAIL

2. When did the Panama Canal open?
   A. 1914
   B. 1928
   C. 1977
   D. 1999

3. Which of the following statements is true?
   A. Panama has mountains.
   B. Panama is very flat.
   C. Panama is an island.
   D. Panama has many deserts.

4. What moves water from one lock to another?
   A. explosives
   B. ships
   C. technology
   D. gravity

5. Tolls vary depending on
   A. the time of day
   B. the size and shape of the ship
   C. the entrance and the exit
   D. one coast to the other

6. Who operated the Panama Canal before 1977?
   A. Boston
   B. San Francisco
   C. the U.S.
   D. the Republic of Panama

INFERENCE

7. Why is it possible for companies to sell goods at a lower cost?
   A. Companies pay tolls to use the canal.
   B. Companies save time and money by using the canal.
   C. Companies think the canal is a wonder of technology.
   D. Ships can go through the canal every day of the year.

8. How is the Panama Canal like an elevator?
   A. A wall closes behind a ship when it is in a lock.
   B. Water from a river feeds the lake and all the locks.
   C. The locks carry ships up and down again in stages.
   D. Ships enter one side and exit the other side.

VOCABULARY REVIEW

WHICH MEANING?

From Chapter 1: *Gabriela Sabatini: Life after Tennis*

1. What does *fan* mean in this context?

> In 1996, at age 26, Gabriela Sabatini retired from professional tennis. Her fans, other tennis players, and people in Argentina were sad.

   A. fan *(verb)* cool by moving the air
   B. fan *(noun)* a person who admires someone or something
   C. fan *(verb)* spread out

From Chapter 2: *Machu Picchu*

2. What does *held* mean in this context?

> In the center of the village, the Incas built a tall stone column, called *intihuatana*. They held a special ceremony there every year before winter came.

   A. held *(verb)* took something in their arms
   B. held *(verb)* kept in one position by force
   C. held *(verb)* organized an event

From Chapter 3: *The Panama Canal*

3. What does *strip* mean in this context?

> On a map, Panama looks like a thin strip of land connecting Central and South America.

   A. strip *(noun)* a narrow piece of something
   B. strip *(verb)* remove something that is covering a surface
   C. strip *(verb)* take something away from someone

WRONG WORD

One word in each group does not fit. Circle the word.

1. glamorous	exciting	wonder	survivor
2. engineer	lock	chamber	elevator
3. decline	feed	wear down	decrease
4. cheap	toll	inexpensive	free
5. talented	skilled	fragile	able
6. series	gravity	group	line

WORDS IN CONTEXT

Fill in the blanks with words from each box.

afford	ancient	career	explosives	guide

1. Tourists visit Machu Picchu to see the _____ ruins.
2. Gabriela Sabatini began her tennis _____ at the age of 14.
3. To break through rock, workers sometimes have to use _____.
4. Our teacher gave us a study _____ to help us understand the chapter.
5. Some professional athletes make a lot of money. They can _____ to buy nice things.

considered	destinations	feed	top	wonder

6. After she won the U.S. Open tournament, Sabatini was the _____ women's tennis player in the world.
7. To make a copy of this letter, I need to _____ paper into the printer.
8. The Panama Canal is amazing! It is a _____ of engineering and technology.
9. Building the Panama Canal was dangerous work. People _____ the builders brave and strong.
10. There are many tourist _____ in South America. Machu Picchu is one of them.

decline	fuel	honor	mystery	varies

11. Professional athletes usually don't have long careers. Their energy and abilities _____, and they have to stop playing sports.
12. Next to the bridge, there is a statue in _____ of the workers who built the bridge.
13. Airplanes and cars need different types of _____ to make them go.
14. No one really knows why the Incas left Machu Picchu. It's a _____.
15. The length of a professional athlete's career _____ from person to person. Each athlete is different.

WORD FAMILIES

Fill in the blanks with words form each box.

survival *(noun)*	survive *(verb)*	survivor *(noun)*

1. In professional sports, an athlete's _____ depends on strength and talent.
2. In the past, it was difficult to _____ disease and war.

| explosion *(noun)* | explosive *(adjective)* | explode *(verb)* |

3. Workers at the Panama Canal had to work with _____ materials to break through the mountains.

4. People heard the _____ of the gas line many miles away.

| variation *(noun)* | various *(adjective)* | vary *(verb)* |

5. A man-made lake feeds the Panama Canal's locks. This was an unusual way to build a canal. It was a _____ of the design of other canals.

6. Experts have _____ ideas about what happened to Machu Picchu. There isn't just one idea.

WRAP IT UP

DISCUSS THE THEME

Read these questions and discuss them with your partner.

1. Who is your favorite Latin American professional athlete (past or present)? Why?

2. Why do you think the Incas built Machu Picchu in a place that is difficult to reach? What are some possible reasons?

3. The Panama Canal changed the way people travel and ship goods.
   • Do you think these changes were all positive (good)?
   • What are some possible negative (bad) effects of the Panama Canal for Latin America?

RESPOND IN WRITING

Look back at the unit and choose the passage you enjoyed the most. Read it again. Write a short summary of the passage.

_____

_____

_____

_____

_____

What do you think is the most interesting thing about this passage, and why? Write a short paragraph.

_____

_____

_____

_____

_____

_____

TRANSPORTATION
MASS TRANSIT

An elevated New York City subway train

CHAPTER 1

◀ Alfred Beach, 1826–1896

Discuss these questions.

1. Have you ever ridden in an elevated train or a subway? Did you enjoy it?
2. Would you rather ride above or below ground? Why?

WORD FOCUS

Match the words with their definitions.

A.

1. equipment ___	**a.** be real; be found in the real world
2. exist ___	**b.** pretend to be someone
3. inventor ___	**c.** a copy of something that is usually smaller than the real thing
4. model ___	**d.** a person who makes something for the first time
5. pose ___	**e.** things needed to carry out an activity

B.

1. secret ___	**a.** a way to fix a problem
2. solution ___	**b.** a type of bus that was pulled by horses
3. trolley ___	**c.** a long hollow pipe
4. tube ___	**d.** something that is not known by other people
5. tunnel ___	**e.** a passage under the ground

SCAN

Guess if this is true or false. Circle *a* or *b*.

London had a subway before New York City did.

a. True   **b.** False

Scan the passage quickly to check your answer.

Alfred Beach: Subway Inventor

Most people think the first subway in New York City opened in 1904, but that isn't true. New York had an earlier subway, but few people have heard of it.

5 In the 1800s, New York City was a very crowded place, and many people had no transportation. Some people rode on horses or in carriages. Most people had to walk or take the **trolley**. 10 But the city was crowded and needed a **solution**.

In this crowded city, trains that ran above ground were an expensive solution. Alfred Beach, an **inventor** 15 and magazine owner, proposed an underground solution. Beach wanted to build a train system under the city.

Beach knew that London, England had an underground train system. This 20 system worked, but smoke from the steam engines made many passengers sick. At that time, there were no electric motors.

Beach had also heard of an 25 underground mail **tube** in London. This tube used air to move mail and packages under the city. It worked very well, so some of the workers decided to have fun. They got into boxes and went for a ride 30 in the tube. Beach heard about their ride and thought this might solve New York's transportation problem. Beach wanted to make a bigger tube and use it to move people from one place to another.

35 Beach created a **model** of his invention for a fair in New York in 1867. The tube for the model was as long as a city street. The model had a subway car with wheels. The car ran on a train track. 40 The car could move from one end of the track to the other and could hold ten passengers. Beach's idea was a success with those who attended the fair. More than 170,000 people rode the model, 45 and Beach's invention received the fair's Gold Medal.

But it wasn't going to be easy to build a whole subway system. **Equipment** for building **tunnels** didn't **exist** at that 50 time. The mayor was against the idea, so Beach decided to build his subway in **secret**.

Where did Beach get the money to build this secret subway? Beach had 55 made money from several inventions. So, he formed a company and said he was building tunnels to transport packages under the streets. The mayor allowed this plan because Beach was going to 60 transport packages, not people.

All of the work was done at night. However, when the project was nearly complete, a reporter **posed** as a worker. Then he wrote about Beach's project. 65 Soon everyone knew about it. Beach opened his subway for everyone to see on February 28, 1870.

Beach's invention was popular with the people, but the mayor asked the 70 governor to stop the project. The subway was never used. The tunnel was closed and forgotten until 1912. Workers discovered it when they were building a tunnel for a new subway. The old subway 75 car was still there, waiting to transport people under the streets of New York.

Read the passage again and answer the questions. Circle your answers.

MAIN IDEA

1. What is the main topic of the passage?
   A. a model subway car at a fair
   B. English workers having fun at work
   C. Beach's plan for a transportation system
   D. New York's transportation problems

DETAIL

2. New York City's first subway opened in
   A. 1850
   B. 1870
   C. 1904
   D. 1912

3. The tube in London was built to transport
   A. horses
   B. mail
   C. people
   D. steam engines

4. Beach's model subway was
   A. one city street long
   B. several streets long
   C. as long as the one in London
   D. five miles (eight km) long

5. Beach's subway was discovered in
   A. 1870
   B. 1904
   C. 1912
   D. 1920

6. Beach built his secret subway with money from
   A. the mayor
   B. several of his inventions
   C. investors
   D. his parents

INFERENCE

7. Why was Beach's project stopped?
   A. It was too difficult to dig tunnels.
   B. The city wasn't ready for subways yet.
   C. The subway cars weren't comfortable.
   D. Beach ran out of money.

8. Why was the work on Beach's project done at night?
   A. Workers are paid less at night.
   B. Beach worked on other projects during the day.
   C. Reporters only worked during the day.
   D. Beach wanted to build his subway in secret.

CHAPTER 2

◀ New York City's subway

PREPARE TO READ

Discuss these questions.

1. Do you think more people drive or take the subway in New York City? Why?

2. In what ways are subways better than cars? In what ways are cars better?

WORD FOCUS

Match the words with their definitions.

A.

1. commuter ___   **a.** going or sent quickly; fast or high-speed
2. connect ___   **b.** the money you pay to travel on a subway, bus, taxi, train, or plane
3. entrance ___   **c.** a person traveling to work or home
4. express ___   **d.** join or link together
5. fare ___   **e.** the door or opening where you go into a place

B.

1. passenger ___   **a.** a person who is living in a place
2. resident ___   **b.** a way from one place to another
3. route ___   **c.** a person who is riding in some type of transportation
4. rush hour ___   **d.** move something or someone from one place to another
5. transport ___   **e.** the time when people travel to work or home

SCAN

Guess if this is true or false. Circle _a_ or _b._

The subway has reduced hours on Sunday.

a. True   **b.** False

Scan the passage quickly to check your answer.

The New York City Subway System

The New York City subway system is the largest subway system in the world. It **transports** people between nearly all areas of New York City. Over 4.3 million
5 people ride the subway every day. Over a billion people use the subway each year. The New York City subway is open 24 hours. There are 468 stations that serve 26 **routes** around the city. That is
10 more than any other subway system in the world.

The subway is popular with New Yorkers. Many people from students to senior citizens depend on the subway to
15 get around. Most people pay their **fare** with a MetroCard. A MetroCard is like a debit card. You just use your MetroCard to travel the underground world of the subway.

20 And the subway is truly another world. You can buy breakfast, have your shoes shined, or get a newspaper from one of the many stores that operate below the city. You can buy flowers for
25 a friend or a snack for your ride. Some stations even have **entrances** that can take you directly into a department store!

Each subway route has a name. It is
30 either a letter or a number. The signs for different subway routes have different colors to make it easy to spot the train that you want. The sign on the subway car also tells you if the train is local or
35 **express**. A local train stops at every station along its route. An express train may only stop at three or four stations. Some trains change from local to express trains during **rush hour**. This helps

40 **passengers** get to work or back home faster.

New York City's subway system started with just one route. Other routes were added as the city grew and more
45 people needed to get into Manhattan. The subway system goes into four sections or boroughs of New York City (the Bronx, Brooklyn, Manhattan, and Queens) but not the fifth borough,
50 Staten Island. The subway **connects** passengers to other train systems and to bus routes as well.

The first working subway line opened in 1904. Over time, additional subway
55 routes were added. Later, these routes were connected so that passengers could go from one route to another without having to pay an additional fare.

Subways make life easier for
60 **commuters** and for tourists who visit the city. Passengers can read, study, or just do nothing while they ride. Taking the subway means less pollution, and passengers don't have to worry about
65 parking or traffic tickets. Thousands of people ride the subway during peak or busy hours from Monday through Friday. The subway operates on the weekend as well, though the hours of service are
70 reduced on Saturday and Sunday.

Subway routes can take passengers to the airport as well as to a baseball game. The system is so complete that many New York City **residents** don't
75 even bother to own a car. For the price of a cup of coffee, you can enter this underground world and take a trip around the city of New York.

Read the passage again and answer the questions. Circle your answers.

MAIN IDEA

1. What is the main topic of the passage?
   A. the New York Subway MetroCard
   B. senior citizens and students on the subway
   C. things you can buy on the subway
   D. the subway system in New York City

DETAIL

2. A train that does **not** stop at every station is called
   A. a local
   B. an express
   C. a rushed train
   D. a Metro

3. The signs for the different subway routes
   A. have pictures of the street above
   B. use special symbols for each route
   C. are different colors
   D. all of the above

4. What can you buy underground?
   A. a shoeshine
   B. food
   C. flowers
   D. all of the above

5. People who ride subways are called
   A. passengers
   B. tourists
   C. residents
   D. New Yorkers

6. When the subway system started,
   A. there were 468 stations
   B. there was one route
   C. there were a billion passengers
   D. there was a department store

INFERENCE

7. Taking the subway means less pollution because
   A. passengers aren't driving cars
   B. subway cars run on energy from the sun
   C. passengers can read while they are riding
   D. subway cars only run during rush hour

8. It isn't necessary to own a car in New York City because
   A. the subways and buses are free
   B. the streets are too narrow for most cars
   C. car owners pay more taxes
   D. good public transportation is available

CHAPTER 3

A high-speed train

Discuss these questions.

1. Have you ever ridden on a high-speed train?
2. What countries have this type of train?

WORD FOCUS

Match the words with their definitions.

A.

1. attract ___	**a.** products
2. distance ___	**b.** cause interest
3. goods ___	**c.** not modern; related to old ideas or products
4. outdated ___	**d.** buy
5. purchase ___	**e.** the amount of space between two places or points

B.

1. reduce ___	**a.** with an even, comfortable movement
2. replace ___	**b.** make less or smaller
3. smooth ___	**c.** going through a place
4. traffic ___	**d.** take the place of something or someone
5. via ___	**e.** cars, trucks, buses that are on a road

SCAN

Guess if this is true or false. Circle *a* or *b*.

The Japanese high-speed train began service in 1981.

a. True   **b.** False

Scan the passage quickly to check your answer.

High-Speed Trains

In the 19th century, trains were the best way to travel long **distances** over land. Trains were fast and convenient. Trains were also quite comfortable, many with sleeping cars and dining cars. However, in the 20th century, airplanes **replaced** trains for long-distance travel. Airplanes were even faster and more convenient than trains for most travel. Trains still transported **goods** over long distances, but passenger trains were mainly for local commuting.

Today, however, high-speed trains are **attracting** passengers again. France has a train called the TGV. TGV is French for "Train a Grande Vitesse," which means high-speed train. Typically, a TGV train operates at speeds up to 186 miles per hour (300 kilometers per hour). The ride is fast, and it is also very **smooth**. Passengers can travel from Paris to Marseilles in only four hours.

The first section of the TGV line between Paris and Lyon was completed in 1981. Since then, France has added several more TGV lines and has **purchased** more TGV train cars. This train system has worked well in France. Some TGV trains travel to other countries in Europe, such as Belgium. Passengers can go between the two capitals, Paris and Brussels, in just 90 minutes. Passengers can also travel much faster by TGV than by car.

The first country to have a high-speed train was Japan. The "Shinkansen" or "bullet" train offers a fast, smooth ride between Tokyo and other major cities. This train operates at speeds up to 130 mph (210 kmh) and can travel between Tokyo and Osaka in just three hours. The first high-speed train route in Japan began in 1964. Now this train system connects many cities in Japan.

It is true that the fare on a high-speed train is more expensive than on a regular train. If a passenger wants to save time, a high-speed train is a good choice. If price is the issue, a regular train is less expensive. Both types of train still usually cost less than an airplane to travel the same distance.

Today, several European countries have some kind of high-speed train. South Korea and the United States also have high-speed trains.

In the United States, a high-speed train called Acela operates from Boston to Washington, D.C. **via** New York City. This route is popular because passengers arrive directly in the center of each of these major cities. The Acela trains are faster than regular trains, partly because they stop in fewer cities along the route. But the Acela trains don't travel as fast as high-speed trains in other countries. The train tracks along the route are designed for older types of trains. Because of these older tracks, the Acela trains have to travel more slowly.

Many of these high-speed train lines have **reduced** air **traffic** between cities. Increased train travel will also help reduce crowding at airports. What once seemed to be an **outdated** form of transportation is now in style again.

Read the passage again and answer the questions. Circle your answers.

MAIN IDEA

1. What is the main topic of the passage?

    A. faster type of airplanes

    B. faster types of trains

    C. the need for more highways

    D. countries where people like to travel fast

DETAIL

2. High-speed trains offer

    A. a dangerous ride

    B. an uncomfortable ride

    C. a slow ride

    D. a smooth ride

3. The "bullet" train is found in

    A. France

    B. Belgium

    C. Japan

    D. the U.S.

4. What is the French train called?

    A. VGT

    B. GVT

    C. TVG

    D. TGV

5. How fast can the high-speed trains travel?

    A. 90 miles per hour (144 kmh)

    B. 186 miles per hour (298 kmh)

    C. 300 miles per hour (480 kmh)

    D. 1,981 miles per hour (3,170 kmh)

6. Which of these is probably least expensive?

    A. a ticket on a regular train

    B. a ticket on a high-speed train

    C. a ticket on an airplane

    D. a ticket on a private jet

INFERENCE

7. People in Europe

    A. have had high-speed trains for only ten years

    B. like plane travel more than train travel

    C. use trains only for commuting to work

    D. use high-speed trains frequently

8. It is possible that Acela trains will

    A. travel faster on different tracks

    B. no longer stop in New York City

    C. replace subways and buses

    D. become less expensive than regular trains

VOCABULARY REVIEW

CROSSWORD PUZZLE

Complete the crossword using the clues.

ACROSS

2. Buy.

4. A person who lives in a place.

5. Move someone or something to another place.

7. A passage under the ground.

8. Through a place.

DOWN

1. Fast or high-speed.

3. Cause interest.

4. A way from one place to another.

6. Something not modern is _____.

WRONG WORD

One word in each group does not fit. Circle the word.

1. connect	express	join	link
2. rush	hurry	reduce	fast
3. transport	move	carry	fare
4. connect	goods	via	through
5. outdated	smooth	comfortable	even
6. passenger	rider	commuter	smooth

Fill in the blanks with words from each box.

equipment	express	posed	residents	tunnel

1. Beach needed the right _____ to complete his project.
2. Many _____ of the city use public transportation.
3. The workers dug a secret _____ under the city.
4. The thief _____ as a salesman.
5. _____ trains are faster than regular trains.

commuters	connects	distances	entrance	trolleys

6. Some _____ travel 50 miles (80 km) to work every day.
7. Airplanes can fly long _____ in a short period of time.
8. The _____ to the tunnel was a small door.
9. The bridge _____ the two cities.
10. Some cities still have _____, but they run on electricity.

fare	goods	replaced	smooth	traffic

11. The top of that desk is very _____.
12. There was a lot of _____ on the street.
13. He _____ his old computer with a new one.
14. Trains transport both _____ and passengers.
15. What is the _____ from New York to Boston?

WORD FAMILIES

Fill in the blanks with words from each box.

invent *(verb)*	invention *(noun)*	inventor *(noun)*

1. Beach was a successful _____.
2. One _____ of Beach's was an important part of the typewriter.

| connect (verb) | connection (noun) | connecting (adjective) |

3. The inventor tried to find a _____ between the two ideas.

4. The passenger took a _____ train.

| commute (verb) | commuter (noun) | commute (noun) |

5. He has a long _____ every day.

6. The lawyer has to _____ between New York and Washington twice a week.

WRAP IT UP

DISCUSS THE THEME

Read these questions and discuss them with your partner.

1. Why do people work far away from their homes?

2. Are there ways to make the daily commute more enjoyable?

3. What are some ways to reduce the cost of traveling or commuting?

4. What should the government do to keep public transportation less expensive?

5. Is it better to build more airports or more high-speed trains?

6. Would it be a good idea to have more subways? Why or why not?

RESPOND IN WRITING

Look back at the unit and choose the passage you enjoyed the most. Read it again. Write a short summary of the passage.

_____

_____

_____

_____

_____

What do you think is the most interesting thing about this passage, and why? Write a short paragraph.

_____

_____

_____

_____

_____

_____

ESSENTIAL READING SKILLS: ANSWER KEY AND EXPLANATIONS

WHAT TO DO BEFORE YOU READ

A.

1. *Possible answer*: An African American man is shown in old-fashioned clothes. The second photo shows an eclipse of the sun.

2. *Possible answer*: Maybe the passage will be about this man and eclipses.

B.

1. The caption on the left tells us that his name is Benjamin Banneker. It also has the dates 1731–1806. The caption on the right tells us that this is a solar eclipse.

2. He is no longer living. The first date is the year he was born; the second date is the year he died.

3. Answers will vary.

4. A solar eclipse occurs when the moon passes between the Earth and the sun.

C.

1. The title names Benjamin Banneker, so the passage is about a person.

2. Benjamin Banneker is named in the title and is the person in the painting. The title says he is an astronomer; this relates to the photo of the eclipse.

3. *Possible answer*: The passage will be about Benjamin Banneker. He must have been an astronomer.

D.

1. 10   **2.** 1

E.

1. The first paragraph

2. The last paragraph

WHAT TO DO WHILE YOU READ

A.

Does it have dialogue? <u>No</u>

Is it a story? <u>No</u>

Does it have technical vocabulary? <u>Yes</u>

Does it have charts and diagrams? <u>No</u>

Is it academic or professional? <u>Yes</u>

Does it have dates and events in a person's life? <u>Yes</u>

Is it a biography? <u>Yes</u>

B.

1. slavery, colonies, astronomy, instruments, observe, eclipse, almanac, accurate, surveyor, plan

2. *solar*

3. 1731; April 14, 1789; 1791, 1806

4. 21, 40 years, two days, 200 years ago

5. Maryland; American colonies; United States; Washington, D.C.

6. Benjamin Banneker, Thomas Jefferson, George Washington, Pierre Charles L'Enfant

C.

True. The passage says that Banneker knew George Washington and that Washington asked Banneker to work on the new capital. (see lines 54–58)

> TIP: Remember to decide what type of information to look for.

D.

1. What is the main topic of the passage?

A is not correct. This is a detail.

B is the correct answer.

C is not correct. These are two of the famous men that Banneker knew.

D is not correct. This is too general. The passage is only about one astronomer.

E.

2. Benjamin Banneker was

A is not correct. This is one of the correct answers, but **B** and **C** are also correct.

B is not correct. This is one of the correct answers, but **A** and **C** are also correct.

C is not correct. This is one of the correct answers, but **A** and **B** are also correct.

D is correct. This is the correct answer. It includes the information in **A**, **B**, and **C**.

> **TIP:** Don't choose the first answer that is correct. Read all of the choices.

3. What was special about the clock that Banneker made?

A is not correct. The clock ran for 40 years, not 200 years.

B is the correct answer. Banneker's clock was made only of wood.

C is not correct. The passage does not say that it was the first clock in the U.S.

D is not correct. The passage does not say he gave the clock to anyone.

> **TIP:** Eliminate any choices that you know are clearly wrong.

4. What did Banneker publish?

A is not correct. A newspaper is not mentioned.

B is not correct. Banneker worked on the plans for Washington, D.C., but the passage does not say he wrote a book about it.

C is the correct answer. Banneker published an almanac.

D is not correct. The passage mentions slavery, but the passage does not say Banneker wrote a book about it.

> **TIP:** Sometimes you need to look at details from different places in the passage.

F.

5. Which of the following is **not** true?

A is not correct. Mathematicians, astronomers, and Thomas Jefferson are mentioned in the passage. We can infer that they all admired his accuracy.

B is not correct. Banneker drew L'Enfant's plan after L'Enfant took it to France. From this we can infer that Banneker understood L'Enfant's plan.

C is the correct answer. Jefferson admired Banneker's accurate predictions about eclipses, but we cannot infer from the passage that Jefferson predicted an eclipse.

D is not correct. Washington asked Banneker to be a surveyor on the team. From this we can infer that Washington thought Banneker was a good surveyor.

> **TIP:** Be careful of words like *not.*

6. What can we say about Banneker?

A is the correct answer. Banneker's calculations were very accurate. From this we can infer that he was a very good mathematician.

B is not correct. The passage says this was the time of slavery and that his mother was a free woman. From this we can infer that Banneker was born during, not after slavery.

C is not correct. The passage does not say how rich Banneker was. He may have been rich, but we cannot infer that he was the richest African American.

D is not correct. The passage says only that his mother was a free woman. His grandmother taught him to read and write, but we cannot infer that his mother was dead.

> **TIP:** Be careful of superlatives.

G.

1. A This was the time of **slavery** in the American colonies, <u>but</u> Banneker's mother was a <u>free woman</u>.

2. B He used instruments such as the <u>telescope</u> to **observe** the stars and planets. He <u>noticed</u> how the stars and planets moved.

3. C Banneker's predictions about eclipses were **accurate**. His predictions were <u>correct</u> because he made <u>careful calculations</u>.

4. Banneker was interested in astronomy, <u>the study of the stars and the planets</u>.

5. He used instruments such as the <u>telescope</u> to observe the stars.

6. An almanac is usually published <u>annually</u>, or <u>yearly</u>.

7. That is how he predicted that a *solar* eclipse would happen on April 14, 1789. Many . . . had predicted a different date for this eclipse <u>of the sun</u>.

VOCABULARY INDEX

A
accomplish **17**
adapt **6**
admire **32**
adventure **59**
afford **87**
allergy **23**
alter **23**
amazing **62**
ancient **90**
architect **32**
aroma **20**
arrest **73**
assassinate **48**
assistant **59**
associate **79**
attract **107**
austere **76**

B
balance **9**
bead **3**
boast **76**
bring out **87**
broadcast **48**

C
cactus **62**
canyon **62**
capture **59**
career **87**
carve **3**
ceremony **65**
charge **59**
charity **20**
choir **45**
claim **37**
clap **51**
client **34**
climate **62**
closet **34**
column **90**
community **20**
commuter **104**
compete **37**
competition **45**
complicated **76**

compliment **45**
concept **3**
condense **34**
conductor **45**
connect **104**
consider **87**
contact **9**
courage **45**
craft **3**
crime **73**
criticism **79**
crop **23**
cross **79**

D
dangerous **62**
decline **87**
decorate **59**
depend on **9**
design **32**
development **23**
distance **107**
dramatic **62**
drown **76**
dust **65**

E
enemy **34**
engineer **93**
engineered **23**
entrance **104**
equipment **101**
exist **3**
explorer **59**
explosive **93**
express **104**
exquisite **17**

F
fare **104**
federal **79**
feed **93**
festival **51**
flexible **32**
form **3**
founder **20**
fragile **90**

free **48**
fuel **90**
function **34**

G
gangster **73**
gem **65**
generation **9**
generous **20**
genetic **23**
glamorous **87**
goods **107**
gospel **51**
gourmet **17**
gravity **93**
guide **90**

H
hall **51**
harmony **34**
harsh **6**
hearth **6**
height **37**
hidden **65**
high-rise **32**
historic **48**
hold **79**
honor **48**
hymn **51**

I
ideal **76**
illegal **73**
improve **79**
in honor of **87**
inauguration **45**
individually **20**
inequality **45**
infamous **76**
influence **32, 51**
inmate **73**
inspire **17**
install **34**
inventor **101**
investigate **79**
isolated **9**

J

journey 93
joyful 17

L

legacy 17
legendary 59
line 87
lively 51
local 51
lost 90

M

man-made 93
massive 48
masterpiece 17
mine 65
mineral 65
model 101
monument 48
mural 3
mystery 90

N

nutrition 23

O

opponent 23
original 9
outdated 107

P

partition 32
passenger 104
peak 73
perform 65
performance 45
permanent 6
petroglyph 62
physician 34
port 51
pose 101
pouch 6
pride 37
prison 76
progress 37
proud 87

proverb 17
purchase 107
put away 73

Q

quest 59

R

raise 90
rare 6
recipe 20
reduce 107
release 73
remote 3
replace 107
resident 104
resistant 23
rest 37
rhythm 51
rival 73
route 104
ruins 62
rush hour 104

S

scarce 9
screen 34
secret 101
segregation 45
series 93
sew 3
shallow 48
share 9
shortcut 93
skin 6
skyscraper 32
slab 34
slavery 48
smooth 107
solution 101
souvenir 20
spa 20
spirit 9
spring 65
statue 48
status 37
symbol 37

spire 37
stonemason 32
structure 6
suit 6
supplies 3
support 79
supposedly 65
survive 6
survivor 90
surround 76

T

talent 45
temporarily 37
toll 93
top 87
tower 32
track down 79
traffic 107
transfer 76
transport 104
trap 9
treasure 59
treasure hunter 59
trolley 101
trust 79
tube 101
tunnel 101

U

unimaginable 17
unique 20
universal 17
unsuccessful 65

V

vary 93
via 107
virus 23

W

wealthy 73
wear down 90
wilderness 62
wonder 62

COMMON IRREGULAR VERBS

INFINITIVE	SIMPLE PAST	PAST PARTICIPLE
be	was/were	been
become	became	become
begin	began	begun
blow	blew	blown
break	broke	broken
bring	brought	brought
build	built	built
buy	bought	bought
catch	caught	caught
choose	chose	chosen
come	came	come
cost	cost	cost
cut	cut	cut
do	did	done
draw	drew	drawn
drive	drove	driven
eat	ate	eaten
fall	fell	fallen
feel	felt	felt
find	found	found
fly	flew	flown
forget	forgot	forgotten
freeze	froze	frozen
get	got	gotten
give	gave	given
go	went	gone/been
grow	grew	grown
hang	hung	hung
have	had	had
hear	heard	heard
hold	held	held
hurt	hurt	hurt
keep	kept	kept
know	knew	known
lay	laid	laid
leave	left	left

INFINITIVE	SIMPLE PAST	PAST PARTICIPLE
let	let	let
light	lit/lighted	lit/lighted
lose	lost	lost
make	made	made
mean	meant	meant
meet	met	met
pay	paid	paid
put	put	put
read	read	read
ride	rode	ridden
ring	rang	rung
run	ran	run
say	said	said
see	saw	seen
sell	sold	sold
send	sent	sent
set	set	set
show	showed	shown
sing	sang	sung
sit	sat	sat
sleep	slept	slept
speak	spoke	spoken
spend	spent	spent
stand	stood	stood
steal	stole	stolen
swim	swam	swum
take	took	taken
teach	taught	taught
tear	tore	torn
tell	told	told
think	thought	thought
throw	threw	thrown
understand	understood	understood
wear	wore	worn
win	won	won
write	wrote	written